FREEMASONRY—A RELIGION?

FREEMASONRY
–a religion?

JOHN LAWRENCE

KINGSWAY PUBLICATIONS
EASTBOURNE

ISBN 0 86065 447 8

Unless otherwise indicated, biblical quotations are from
the New American Standard Bible
© The Lockman Foundation 1960, 1962, 1963, 1968,
1971, 1972, 1973

Front cover design by Vic Mitchell

Printed in Great Britain for
KINGSWAY PUBLICATIONS LTD
Lottbridge Drove, Eastbourne, E. Sussex BN23 6NT by
Richard Clay Ltd, Bungay, Suffolk
Typeset by CST, Eastbourne, E. Sussex.

Contents

Author's Note

As this book went to press I received details of the Grand Lodge meeting held on 11th June 1986 at which it was proposed that the traditional physical penalties be removed from the obligations and that they be transferred to another part of the ceremonies as part of the traditional history. There was, I understand, a very full and free debate, in which anyone present was allowed to contribute. The proposal was carried by a large majority.

The situation is that it is now mandatory that the traditional physical penalties be removed from the obligations and all lodges are required to comply with this ruling. It remains to be seen how this is to be implemented and whether all lodges will comply since it could render obsolete most if not all previously published masonic rituals. It would seem likely that the decision taken is merely to make compulsory the permissive variations passed in December 1964. However, there is a substantial element within the craft who will not welcome this decision. It could be that they will stand firm and cause a deep rift, but whatever the outcome the savage oaths will remain in the ceremonies, albeit in a less threatening and prominent position.

Acknowledgements

I had never realized how long a venture such as this takes. My love and thanks for the patience of the people of Saint Justus, who have had to be without their vicar. Particular thanks to Marion for such prompt and accurate typing of manuscripts. Special love to Peter and Sarah when Dad has had his mind elsewhere and to Dawn for being simply the best wife in the world.

Most of all I thank God the Father of our Lord Jesus Christ, for saving me and giving me his Spirit. This book is given back to him for his glory.

Introduction

For many years there has been an uneasy relationship between the church and freemasonry (called by its members 'the craft'). Secrecy can breed either smug satisfaction or suspicion, depending on whether you are a member or not. This strained relationship does not only exist between the church and the craft; it is found in many marriages. The mason is obliged to keep secret virtually everything that goes on and his wife may strongly resent this refusal to share and this apparent lack of trust.

From an early age I was aware of this tension. My grandfather on my mother's side, a policeman, was a constable all his life. He blamed his lack of promotion entirely on free-masonry. His contention was that many far less able men than himself received promotion merely because they exchanged the right handshake.

Whether he was right we will never know.

Of course, it is easy to look for scapegoats to blame for our own lack of success but three things I know: firstly, he was a highly respected 'copper'—people I have met who knew him have consistently told me that; secondly, he was a man of principle and would not join an organization which he believed to be wrong merely for personal gain; thirdly, he was quite bitter about it. On my father's side, my two uncles were masons. One I idolized as a youngster. He had everything I wanted to make a success of life. His death by suicide shook me deeply. I have come to realize that, like so many, though he seemed to have so much, in reality he did not have enough to make him value his own life. My other uncle I respect greatly. He has been Lodge Master and chaplain of his lodge. We talk often about the craft and the cross. My family situation is not, I suspect, untypical.

It was a conversation that I had about twelve years ago with a neighbour, a kindly man, which caused many thoughts to crystallize. He spoke about God in some depth, using words and expressions that I had occasionally heard other masons use. I knew him to be a keen mason and the thought struck me, 'I wonder if he derives his appreciation of God, which he expresses in such a strange way, from masonry?' I gather that I was not alone in my amazed curiosity. C. Penney Hunt writes:

> In the course of many years' work in the Christian Ministry, I had become increasingly conscious of a lack of support from that section of my congregations, which was associated with the Craft. Not that they opposed my appeals; they simply ignored them. It was obvious that their heart was elsewhere. Many times had I asked myself—What subtle influence is affecting these men? So much so that I resolved to find out. And no one can be more amazed than myself at the discoveries made.[1]

Four years later, while I was at theological college, I decided to major on a comparative study of Christianity and freemasonry, purely to satisfy my own curiosity. As I researched I was reminded of conversations and attitudes that I had experienced with masons. For ten years I had worked in the banking world where it was not difficult to discover the masons. Each bank manager I served under was a mason.

My research took me into many strange and interesting situations. I was greatly encouraged by the helpfulness and openness of many of the masons I met. I was even able to use Grand Lodge library for a time until they became aware that my conclusions were not particularly favourable! I was surprised, too, at the relative ease of obtaining information. I have never found anyone to be knowingly misleading.

There was great interest at college and in the end I had to make fifty copies of my thesis. What had begun as a personal inquiry into the nature of belief within freemasonry, gradually grew. The Church of England Newspaper heard that I had done this research and asked me to write some articles. I understand that the articles met with an unprecedented response, so they were repeated. Following this, London Weekend Television contacted me about making a programme for *Credo* and then came newspapers, publishers, radio and television and many requests to speak. I found myself being called 'an expert'. Stephen Knight contacted me early in his research for *The Brotherhood*,[2] but his and my work, though within the same subject, were very different in emphasis. He was more concerned with corruption and individuals. I saw it as my calling to inform people of the nature of masonic belief and the incompatibility of Christianity and freemasonry. I wanted to show that any mason who also wishes to follow Christ and receive the blessings of eternal life must live a life of compromise. My overwhelming desire was to help men to be free to discover the fullness of the true God.

I

Why the concern?

Is freemasonry a religion? If freemasonry is just an organization, then one can debate whether or not a Christian should
be a member and take part in the many rituals, ceremonies
and oaths that form such a large part of freemasonry. Even
so, as the later chapters of this book show, we have enough
evidence about what takes place in these ceremonies to support the case that it would be extremely unwise for Christians to become involved with freemasonry. If, on the other
hand, it can be shown that rather than just being a society,
freemasonry is in fact a religion in the true sense of the word,
then freemasonry and Christianity must be mutually exclusive.

It will be shown later that freemasonry would claim to
impart special knowledge to its members whereby they can
move along a progressive path to the throne of God. But a
Christian believes we can only approach God through
Christ. The late Stephen Knight, author of the best selling
book *The Brotherhood*, himself not a practising Christian at
the time, saw the problem very clearly. In a phone-in on a
local radio station with the Rev. Gerry Moate, he asked if he

could respond to a question initially addressed to Mr Moate. 'Christians believe,' he said, 'that God can only be approached through Christ: masons do not. The two cannot be compatible.'

Having studied freemasonry for a number of years, I now believe with all my heart that it draws many men who are spiritually hungry but who are being fed a welter of untruths which amount to an elaborate web of religious deception. It implies that it offers them something that their church isn't able to give them, but their spiritual hunger can never be satisfied in this way. The world view that freemasonry imparts obviates the need for a saviour, and therefore they will never find peace with God.

Jesus had no truck with man-made religion, in fact he denounced it in word and deed. He spoke out against the sham, pretence and hypocrisy of the religious leaders of the time and overthrew the tables of the money changers in the temple precincts. He could not use the religious people in the foundation of his church. In the sermon on the mount he affirmed that man cannot serve two masters—he must either serve God or mammon, the divine, or the human but not both.

Freemasonry has gone to considerable lengths to play down its religious side, particularly since the Protestant churches in England have shown a growing concern about their members' allegiance. It also tries to dismiss criticism on the grounds that those on the outside cannot know what is involved in the secret ceremonies and rites. However, it is impossible to keep secret the rites of any organization which has in excess of 300,000 members especially as their allegedly secret rituals can be purchased in retail outlets or through the post. It is not at all difficult to find men who have been involved in freemasonry and some are very willing to talk about what goes on behind the lodge doors, in spite of the oath of secrecy which they have sworn.

It is significant that within our society the whole question of freemasonry is under scrutiny. Several unions, organizations and interest groups are currently considering the desirability of membership and are questioning the compatibility of freemasonry with their beliefs or ethics. When I began my research in 1977 very little was being published about freemasonry. Most people understood it to be a highly respectable organization, essentially secret. Such secrecy gave rise to occasional jokes and gestures but little real concern. Since that time, however, there has been a marked change of attitude both within freemasonry and throughout society in general. Whereas there had been an unhealthy fear of freemasonry largely based, I believe, on the hidden power of this secret organization to damage the livelihood or reputation of any individual who questioned it in any way, there is now a growing openness on both sides, which I did not consider possible even five years ago.

Up until about twenty years ago it was possible to find out who was a member of the craft since under the 1799 Unlawful Societies Act each lodge was required to submit an annual return of names, addresses and descriptions of members to the local Clerk of the Peace. However, the Criminal Law Act 1967 (c.58) changed all that. Most masons welcomed this extra form of secrecy or privacy, possibly seeing it as a vindication of the craft. It gave an added appeal to membership—no one could be found out! What had been an important safety valve within a democratic society had been taken away by parliamentary legislation. I think it unlikely that anyone, least of all Grand Lodge, the governing body of freemasonry in this country, could have foreseen how it would work against and tend to undermine the credibility of the craft.

The continuing public concern has caused Grand Lodge to do a complete re-think in the past three years in an effort to restore its respectable image. Prior to this it had responded to pressure from within as a direct result of Walton Hannah's revelations about the nature of masonic oaths and their undesirability for Christians.[1] As a result, some lodges do not force members to take the traditional oaths (see chapter 7), but allow alternative forms of wording which merely refer obliquely to the penalties.

Not only in society in general, but in particular in all the main churches over the last ten years there has been a growing concern about the true nature of masonic belief. People are asking questions: Is it a religion? Does freemasonry obviate the need for Christ? Do masons worship the same God as Christians? Does masonry imply eternal salvation by good or charitable works? How can one organization claim to unite men of all religions without compromising any one of them? Is it occult? What is this JAH-BUL-ON deity in freemasonry? There is also a growing anxiety about the secrecy and the harbouring of activity which may not be in the public interest.

My concern is especially with the spiritual blindfold that freemasonry puts across a man's mind to prevent him seeing the truth about Christ and to stop him receiving the fullness of the Spirit. I know that I am in no way alone in this. Just recently I was at a clergy chapter in Kent where most of the ministers referred to difficult pastoral situations which they attributed to masonic influence. To be fair to Grand Lodge, they have held several meetings at which they have attempted to make clear the craft's position with regard to religion, even going to the unprecedented extreme of publishing a leaflet which states that they certainly do not see themselves as a religion. However, this has not really done anything to allay concern.

Eminent masons have gone on record as saying that freemasonry is a religion. Twice I have been involved in television programmes about freemasonry. In the first a Jewish rabbi, and in the second a Methodist lay preacher, in speaking about the value of the craft for bringing together men of different religions, described them as being 'one in the faith'!

2

Basic masonic beliefs

The fact that freemasonry has no systematized statement of beliefs is frequently cited by Grand Lodge, and more recently by those apparently speaking on the craft's behalf, as proof that it is not a religion. However, beliefs do not have to be put into formal doctrinal statements. Part of the purpose of this book is to set out something of the beliefs of freemasonry as they are published in the craft rituals to which all would-be masons must submit if they are to gain acceptance and recognition.

English freemasonry, as opposed to Orient freemasonry, is based on the supposition that a man believes in a supreme being. The first charge given to a freemason begins thus:

> A Mason is obliged, by his tenure, to obey the moral law; and if he rightly understand the art he will never be a stupid atheist nor an irreligious libertine . . . . Let a man's religion or mode of worship be what it may, he is not excluded from the order, provided he believe in the glorious architect of heaven and earth . . . .

This is the first condition of admission into the craft and is stated as essential, admitting no compromise. The former

Bishop of Woolwich, Michael Marshall, stated in the June 1981 *Credo* (LWT) programme on the compatibility of Christianity and freemasonry that such a 'lowest common denominator' view of God 'emptied him of all meaning' and could not in any way be considered a valid Christian interpretation.

The nature of the required belief in a god is not defined further prior to initiation. However, it is expected that a mason:

> . . . practise the sacred duties of morality. Masons unite with the virtuous of every persuasion in the firm and pleasing bond of fraternal love; they are taught to view the errors of mankind with compassion, and to strive, by the purity of their own conduct, to demonstrate the superior excellence of the faith they may profess.[1]

It is significant that the basis of masonic fraternity is the assumption that there are 'virtuous' in every system of belief. It is a similarly implied tenet of the craft that there is some virtue in every sacred volume for:

> The Bible, referred to by Freemasons as the Volume of the Sacred Law, is always open in the Lodges. Every Candidate is required to take his Obligation on that book or on the Volume which is held by his particular creed to impart sanctity to an oath or promise taken upon it.[2]

In practice, lodges have open the sacred volumes which relate to all the members of that particular lodge, implying that all are equal.

The 'Volume of Sacred Law' has traditionally been regarded as one of the three 'Great Lights of Freemasonry', the others being the square and the compasses (see chapter 7). Although freemasonry appears to recognize all religions which acknowledge a supreme being, it forbids any discussion of religion within its doors.[3] Some Christians, and members of other faiths, would say that the purpose of this is

to deny them the opportunity of sharing their faith and
Grand Lodge has never contradicted this interpretation.
However, it steadfastly maintains that it is not a religion, nor
a competitor with religion.

It may seem strange to some that a body which professes
not to be a religion nevertheless makes it a normal requirement that every single lodge should have a chaplain, and
certainly at Grand Lodge level, the chaplain is required to
'offer up solemn prayer, suitable to the occasion . . . .'[4]
Grand Lodge counters that this is similar to the armed forces
and most public schools. However, in the forces and public
schools, the chaplain's job is to explain the teaching of Christianity and point those in need to Jesus Christ. My purpose
in this book is to make it plain that in its composition freemasonry fits the standard definitions of a religion, with its
chaplain's explaining the teaching of freemasonry and minis-
tering its own equivalent of the sacraments.

Concern from a Christian standpoint comes firstly from
the fact that, certainly within craft freemasonry, the masonry
enjoyed by the bulk of the membership, Christ is excluded.
Many other organizations such as anglers, numismatists,
friendship and introduction agencies will very likely admit to
this. They however, will not include a high level of ritual
containing supposed knowledge about, and worship of, a
supreme being.

As I said in chapter 1, it would seem from the craft rituals
that all masons are gradually lead to believe that they are
setting out on a progressive path of enlightenment leading to
the throne of God. The mason will be encouraged to think
he can approach God on the grounds of special knowledge
that is given him, continuing good conduct, and participation
in masonic ceremonies. This is in direct contradiction to the
teaching of Christ, who said, 'I am the way, and the truth,
and the life; no one comes to the Father, but through Me'
(John 14:6).

The secrecy of freemasonry is built on a continuing requirement for oaths (or 'obligations', as they are called)
which are sworn as a candidate progresses through the different degrees. These oaths contain graphic descriptions of
the bloodthirsty and usually fatal consequences of divulging
masonic secrets. Several questions are raised by the whole
notion of masonic secrecy. Why is it necessary at all, since it
is freely admitted by those within the craft that the secrets
are inconsequential? Why does the United Grand Lodge
maintain the secrecy when many other parallel Grand
Lodges do not require it, though they use basically the same
rituals? Since masonic rituals can now be obtained by the
general public, why is it still desirable to attempt to keep the
seal of silence by way of either illegal or unenforcible blood
pacts? The traditionalists within freemasonry may simply not
allow these questions to be considered; the grassroots feeling
against change within the craft is a far stronger influence
than, say, the Book of Common Prayer lobby within the
Church of England.

The attitudes of freemasonry towards God, the Bible,
faith and good works, religion and particularly Christ, will be
considered in the following chapters. We shall also draw out
significant aspects of masonic belief as we look at the main
rituals, considering the possibility of compatibility with orthodox Christian doctrine and the wider question of whether
freemasonry itself fulfils the criteria for being a religion.

3

A brief history—creation, evolution and Christian excision

It's amazing that when people look at a new-born baby, almost without exception they comment on the fact that the new offspring looks exactly like one or other parent or some member of the family. If you took a dozen independent visitors, you could be fairly certain that at least half a dozen different similarities would be noticed. There can be many explanations for this—changes caused by natural growth and development, the way the baby is dressed at any particular time or else preconceived ideas in the onlooker, even possibly a degree of seeing what he or she wants to see—and, of course, defects of sight!

The same thing happens when the question of the origin of freemasonry is considered. The whole subject is so vast, and clear derivations are difficult to discern since:

1. the craft has developed in many directions;
2. rituals, passwords and signs have various origins and have to be unpieced like bits of a jigsaw puzzle;
3. records prior to the eighteenth century are few and far between;
4. freemasonry is a secret society, or—as masons would

    have it—a society with secrets;

5.   the investigator himself comes with some preconceived notions, so that interpretation of the limited information available is subjective.

There has been much speculation, and much has been written on the question of masonic history. The theory has been put forward that Adam was the first mason and that many of the best known Old Testament characters were the forerunners of today's leaders. We shall see in the course of this book that great emphasis is put on parts of Old Testament religion and symbolism, but it cannot be argued with any degree of conviction that Adam was its originator—any more, that is, than he was the forerunner of all mankind and thereby, I suppose, of all human institutions.

There are, it is true, varying degrees of similarity between freemasonry and many ancient organizations such as those in Ancient Greece and Egypt, especially in aspects of rites and ceremonies, but this argument has been grossly overstated. Authors such as J. S. M. Ward, who have taken these theories of direct descent far further than the plausible evidence allows, do not have any credibility with the vast majority of masons today.

Knoop and Jones consider that many authors are 'insufficiently aware that the history of building is not the same as the history of freemasonry'.[1] Other historians regarded by most masons today as largely reliable are Pick and Knight, and in this connection they comment:

> Many doctrines belong to vast traditions of humanity of all ages and all parts of the world . . . but there is no convincing evidence to prove the lineal descent from any ancient organization.[2]

They conclude:

> Up to the present time, no even plausible theory of the 'origin' of the Freemasons has been put forward. The reason for this is

probably that the Craft, as we know it, originated among the operative masons of Britain. No doubt it incorporated from the earliest times shreds of ritual, folk-lore and even occult elements of time-immemorial antiquity. But it is almost certainly a British product and of British origin.[3]

Though stone-masonry had been a recognized craft for several centuries earlier, there is no evidence of any internal organization before the fourteenth century. The earliest reference to a lodge (the Vale Royal Abbey Lodge) dates from a manuscript of 1278. Though it is difficult to see how any church, abbey or castle of any size could have been erected with elaborate ornamentation unless some central workshop had existed, it is not insignificant that the earliest reference to apprenticeship dates from 1382. This is in accordance with the great increase in skill, elaborate ornamentation, and general standard of workmanship evident in buildings of that period.

It was from that time that lodges which seem to have begun as workshops, storehouses and places of shelter from inclement weather gradually developed as rest places, sometimes for social purposes as a kind of club. Records of the fifteenth century show how these developed and at the same time provide evidence of lodge rules, conditions of employment and rules of conduct. Though statutes of 1360 and 1425 prohibited the formation of congregations or confederations of masons, the two earliest masonic manuscripts make reference to such assemblies. Thus it seems that from early days these laws were not observed by the craft.

Economic conditions usually gave rise to these organizations which seem to have been formed for the illegal purpose of maintaining or enhancing wages, and protecting the employees' interests. A comparison of wages and the price of food for the period from 1500-1700 shows that the purchasing power of masons' pay fell by 50%—and we think that we are the ones most troubled by inflation! General rules which applied to succeeding groups of workers inevitably existed. These covered tools, hours, holidays and special rewards, but equally inevitably they varied from one locality to another.

It was at that time that the need to maintain standards was realized, especially in Scotland. As the craft became more skilled, it was apparent that the less skilled workers (known as cowans in Scotland) were taking some of the work and thereby not only damaging the livelihood of the masons but also harming their reputation. How far secrecy was used to safeguard a method of identification is uncertain. The Regius and Cooke manuscripts (the oldest masonic documents) seem to indicate that it was skill rather than a password which was the pre-requisite of employment. However, it is clear that by the late seventeenth century a system of recognition by handshake was in evidence.

The 'masonic word' seems to have arisen in Scotland since there tests of skill were not considered sufficient for recognizing a mason. A statute dated 1598 made it a punishable offence to employ or work with 'cowans' whose presence was encouraged by the comparatively easily-worked and readily available freestone. This, coupled with the decreasing volume of work for the church, together with the fact that planning and designing were increasingly carried out by people other than masons (with the advent of architects) caused the masonic fraternity gradually to decline in status and influence. These factors would also have been responsible for the fall in wages referred to above.

No doubt to combat the waning of power, the craft began to move towards widening its appeal and its respectability. Men who were in a more general sense involved in medieval buildings were encouraged to join. Various manuscripts indicate that provision was made for this at the beginning of the sixteenth century and certainly by the mid seventeenth century non-operatives such as mayors, sheriffs and local gentry were members. By 1670 one lodge in Aberdeen is recorded as having only ten operatives out of forty-nine members, and one in Chester three years later had only six operative masons out of twenty-six.

From this time freemasonry began completely to change its character and appeal. From being an operative craft guild it successfully recruited men of social standing and also provided a haven for those who sought a refuge for secret discussion. The late seventeenth and early eighteenth centuries were characterized by a new humanitarian society whose pursuit was knowledge. Partly as a result of puritanical discipline and, in some measure, reaction to the Renaissance and the Reformation, authority was becoming increasingly questioned, especially the authority of the church and her clergy.

The 1689 Act of Toleration disappointed masons, who felt it did not go far enough in giving respectability to the vogue of reason. But, by granting freedom of belief to proponents of deism, a form of religion which holds that God gives the earth its initial start, then leaves it to run its course, the Act did in fact serve as an impetus to the craft. Deism at this time entered its period of greatest activity and widest influence and as men, generally from the upper classes, infiltrated the craft they brought with them the teaching of deism, which thus became the seed-bed of modern freemasonry. Much of the ritual which is present in today's rituals certainly came from this period of free thought. God was seen as impersonal. Reality was the cardinal virtue with revelation supplying merely supplementary information. Mystery and wonder were effectively rejected and Scripture made subordinate to reason. It seems more likely that the origin of today's masonic 'secret' can be found in this period of influence than in the vestiges of the operative craft guild.

By 1717 the operative element was an anachronism and Alec Mellor concludes: 'Many testimonies prove that a taste for the occult sciences has attracted not a few recruits to the

English Lodges.'[4]

It is interesting and significant that the earliest manuscripts relating to freemasonry contain references to the Trinity. As we will see, the craft rituals refer to God alone, but in the Grand Lodge No. 1 manuscript of 1583 there is a clear Christian reference to the Father, Son and Holy Ghost in the prayer of invocation. From the little evidence we have, it would seem that before the transition from operative masonry to speculative, there was a strong Christian backbone to the craft.

The year 1717 is seen by many as the time when modern freemasonry was born. Attempts had been made earlier to organize the craft nationally, but it is at that time that the first roots of the present movement can be seen. Four London lodges resolved to join under a Grand Master and on St John the Baptist's Day (June 24) 1717 Anthony Sayer was appointed Grand Master of masons. Within fourteen years the first royal freemasons had been initiated.

The most influential pioneer of masonry at that time was Dr James Anderson whose small book *Anderson's Constitutions* (1723) has been as much a part of freemasonry as the 39 Articles have been to the Church of England, albeit with a great deal of controversy. The 39 (strange coincidence!) General Regulations which form the chief feature of Anderson's work were based on a code compiled by George Payne during his second Grand Mastership in 1720. Some of the contents of the Constitutions have long been an embarrassment to masons, especially the explanation that freemasonry can be traced back to Adam.

Several parts of the Constitutions are, however, of great significance especially with regard to Anderson's background. Anderson's father had been a member of the Aberdeen Lodge in 1670. About 1702 Anderson was licensed as a minister of the Church of Scotland, moving to London in 1709. His affinity with Scotland continued as he received the degree of Doctor of Divinity in 1731 from Aberdeen University. It is worth noting that the highly reputable historians Knoop and Jones record that Anderson 'at one time had a reputation as a profound Talmudic scholar'.[5] The twelve chapters in the *Book of Constitutions,* trace the history of the craft through many religious figures yet expressly exclude Christ.

Various authors have noted different strains of influence:

> Most important is the introduction of several phrases derived from Scottish operative masonry, including 'Entered Apprentice' and 'Fellow Craft' (the old operative expressions in England having been 'Apprentice' and 'Fellow') although Anderson leaves the word 'Cowan' until his second edition in 1738.
>
> Of 'The Charges of a Freemason' the most striking, and one that, as we shall see, was to have far-reaching consequences, is the first which states that ''tis now thought more expedient only to oblige them (Freemasons) to that Religion to which all men agree, leaving their particular opinions to themselves'. Now in spite of Anderson's explanation that in ancient times masons were charged in every country to be of the religion of that country, this article was definitely an innovation, since the Old Charges have almost without exception a positively Christian character.[6]

Pick and Knight conclude that this was probably written to give retrospective coverage for at least two practising Jews who were admitted in 1721, while contemporary scholars in the Quatuor Coronati Lodge disagree about the meaning and effects of this first charge. One view is that it is a change from Christianity to deism, while another is that it was to ease the masonic path for Dissenters, Anderson being a Presbyterian.

In *X-Rays in Freemasonry,* A. Cowan (probably a tongue-in-cheek pseudonym) sees strong resemblances with the Compagnonnage, the French Hatters and even a connection between the Benedictine ceremony of the reception of a novice and the masonic death rite. However, the main influence, he feels, is that of the Compagnonnage especially with regard to the initiation ceremony (breast uncovered and leg ungartered), the Hiramic legend, the compass and square and the term 'Lewis' (parallel to their term 'louveteau').[7] All this seems to confirm his theory that it was Socinianism, whose objects were to destroy Christianity and substitute rationalism in its place, that gave this movement its impetus. (Loelius Socinius himself had the ambition to build upon the ruins of the Catholic Church, a temple which was to include all creeds, a temple of free thought without dogma, a design worthy of Lucifer himself and at his meetings his followers adopted the paraphernalia of working stonemasons, such as the apron, mallet, square, plumb-line and trowel.)

Cowan's views are certainly corroborated by an 'Encyclical Letter' which appeared in 1893 issued by Adriano Lemmi, the Grand Master of the Grand Orient of Italy, acknowledged then as the 'Supreme Pontiff' of the craft: 'We must not forget that Italy was the real cradle of Freemasonry and had Socinius for its real father. . . .'[8]

Apart from his writings and formative views, Anderson's involvement with freemasonry seems to have been slight. It is true that his work was amended and revised and his craft history initially extended, but by the latter part of the century it was so ridiculed that it was dropped altogether. However, the seeds had been sown—at the very least the strong Christian background to operative masonry began rapidly to wane. By 1725 sixty-four lodges were in existence all over the country and by the following year it was necessary to appoint the first Provincial Grand Masters. In the next two years overseas lodges were constituted in Bengal, Gibraltar and Madrid.

As it developed dissension occurred and by the second half of the eighteenth century a separate organization known as the 'Antients' (the mainstream being known as the 'Moderns') began. A rival Grand Lodge was founded in 1751 —the Antients being, in the main, not dissidents from the Moderns but those who followed ritual and customs more akin to the Irish and Scottish rites. Certainly many of them were unhappy with changes that had occurred in the Moderns' ritual and custom, which opened the craft to men of non-Christian faith, and also the failure to observe the feasts of St John as special masonic festivals. However, within a few years secession from one to the other was not uncommon in both directions. For many years the Moderns were highly resentful of the more artisan influenced Antients since, while in the latter part of the century membership of the Moderns declined, the Antients' membership rapidly increased.

Neither body had a particularly smooth passage. Among the Antients there were considerable dissensions, jealousies and squabbling which, on occasion, led to lodges being expelled, but we do see the beginnings of a drawing together in the 1760s when some, following the example of William Dickey, then Grand Secretary of the Antients, also became 'Modern' Masons. His allegiance to the former was in no way diminished as he subsequently became Deputy Grand Master for two periods, totalling ten years.

However, full union between the two rival parties was not to be completed for another half-century. In the early nineteenth century after various unsuccessful initiatives, influential members of both sides, not least the royal members, entered into fraternal alliances through the Grand Lodges of Scotland and Ireland. Part of the drawing together was no doubt as a result of the Unlawful Societies Act of 1799. Parliament passed this act at the height of the wars of the French Revolution to suppress subversive societies, the effect of the law being to suppress oaths taken unlawfully in such societies. However, as a result of the efforts of the

Duke of Atholl and the Earl of Moira, freemasonry was made exempt. Their only requirement was that lodge secretaries were to make an annual return of names, addresses and descriptions of members to the local Clerk of the Peace. After the Criminal Law Act 1967 this was no longer required.

By 1813 Articles of Union had been prepared, differences in ritual examined, and a new working more akin to the Antients was mutually agreed and ratified. Although the Second Article laid down that 'pure Ancient Masonry consists of three degrees and no more viz. those of the Entered Apprentice, the Fellow Craft and the Master Mason, including the Supreme Order of the Royal Arch', several authors have demonstrated that the amalgamation was not the return to the operative or original masonry that we might be led to believe.

This was particularly evident in its religious dimension.

It is true that the supreme position given to the Bible had disappeared by about 1760, from which time it was regarded as a Great Light, but even non-Christian masonic authors saw this as part of an ongoing situation:

> There is no doubt that all our rituals, the Craft included, underwent revision during the 18th Century. In the case of the Craft Degrees a considerable amount of excision was necessitated by the alteration of the clause in the constitution which changed Masonry from a Christian to a non-Christian basis. This process of excision of all Christian references was not completed until the time of the Treaty of Union in 1813, and one example for England will suffice. Dunckley, in the second half of the 18th Century declared that the 'Blazing Star' meant the star of Bethlehem, which guided the wise men to the infant Christ. In Scotland to this day there still survives a distinct reference to Christ in the Craft Degrees for the VSL is opened by the DC with a quotation from the opening verse of the gospel of St. John—'In the beginning was the Word'—whilst the Lodge is closed with the following quotation from the same source, 'And the Word

was with God.' Now this clearly indicates the existence of a Christian explanation of the lost S. . .s which, though no longer countenanced in the Craft Degrees in England, survives in such degrees as the Rose Croix.[9]

We can thus see that anything Christian was eliminated from the lower degrees and this explains the probable origin of some of the Higher Degrees.[10]

The official history book *Grand Lodge 1717-1967* printed specially to mark the 250th anniversary, seems to confirm this:

After the Union, a certain stiffening of authority . . . was exercised to preserve the ancient landmarks including what may be called the comprehensive attitude towards religions.[11]

There is certainly evidence of considerable activity in other countries which paralleled the de-Christianizing of freemasonry in England and Cowan considers that the Scottish Rite took shape in France about 1740. Twenty years later they were ready for export:

In 1762 Stephen Morin, a Jewish Mason was deputed by Duke Louis de Bourbon, Grand Master of France to go to America to propagate the 25 degrees of the Ancient and Accepted Scottish Rite. . . . The American Masons not only accepted the new degrees but in process of time added to them eight others, raising the total of the Scottish Rite to 33 degrees.[12]

Cowan states that the higher degrees all bear the Hebrew stamp, and, although spoken of by some freemasons as being Christian degrees, 'were capable of satanic and impure interpretations, which they receive in many foreign lodges at the present time'.[13] Cowan's source is Folger's History of the A and A Scottish Rite[14] and it is certainly true that strong Talmudic parallels are discernible within the higher degrees and that degrees that are only open to Christians in this country (and which are indeed regarded as Christian) are, in countries such as the United States, open to all, and thus are subject to any number of interpretations.

The early nineteenth century saw the establishment of several Supreme Councils of the Ancient and Accepted Scottish Rite whose rulers, Cowan claims, can be identified with the start of aggressive warfare against the Catholic Church.

The main split in international freemasonry came in 1877 when the French Grand Orient removed from its Constitutions the need to believe in the Supreme Architect and discontinued the use of the Bible (Volume of Sacred Law) in administering the oath. The Grand Orient claimed that they wanted to accommodate positivists who wished to enter the fraternity without subscribing to a belief in a supreme being and they were at pains to explain that this was not tantamount to an endorsement of atheism, even appointing a French Protestant pastor to explain their action. However, English and American Grand Lodges regarded this as heretical and they, and other Anglo-Saxon lodges, withdrew formal recognition. Since that time very little of note has taken place in freemasonry. The emphasis on royal patronage has been maintained and in the years 1936-7 both Edward VIII and George VI were appointed Pro Grand Master with the latter becoming Grand Master. This was followed by the institutions of H.M. King Christian of Denmark (Pro G M 1946), King Gustav V of Sweden (Pro G M 1947), King Gustav VI of Sweden (Pro G M 1966) and the initiation of the Duke of Edinburgh (December 5 1952). The Duke has taken little or no part in the craft since 1953. The Duke of Kent has been Grand Master since 1967.

The great wealth that is part and parcel of the craft was ably demonstrated in the Masonic Million Memorial Fund for the Peace Memorial for which on one day at a meeting held at Olympia more than £826,000 was collected or promised (August 8 1925). The building was begun in 1928 and completed in 1933. Built at the junctions of Great Queen Street, Drury Lane and Long Acre, in the centre of London this Cathedral (or Grand Lodge Temple, as part is called), the headquarters of English freemasonry, is 120 feet long, 90 feet wide and 62 feet high. Its splendour is still apparent today, a testimony to masonic charity.

4

The Church of Rome

As little as ten years ago, it was widely understood in masonic circles that Roman Catholics were not permitted by their Church to belong to the craft. This was accepted as fact by the vast majority of masons, many of whom saw it as sheer prejudice, not understanding the reasons for it. There is now a widespread belief that the position has been reversed and that the Church of Rome does not restrict its members from becoming masons. This is not true. In conjunction with the publication of the revised Code of Canon Law in November 1983, the Congregation for the Doctrine of the Faith issued a statement which affirmed that Catholics who join the freemasons commit 'a serious sin' since masonic principles are 'irreconcilable with the Church's doctrine'. It goes on to declare that membership of organizations of freemasons 'remains prohibited by the Church' and that Catholics who violate this prohibition commit a 'serious sin' and 'may not approach Holy Communion'. It continues: 'Local ecclesiastical authorities do not have the faculty to pronounce a judgment on the nature of Masonic associations which might include a diminution of the above-mentioned judgment.'

The Vatican's condemnation of freemasonry and its attitude that the Church and the craft are irreconcilable in their
basic doctrine is no new phenomenon, it goes back nearly
250 years. Clement XII, acknowledged by his critics as being
an excessively tolerant, gentle and accommodating pope,
was uncompromising in his attitude to freemasonry and its
potential ability to undermine the faith of the Church. In his
papal encyclical of 1738 he concluded:

> . . . to prevent the hearts of the simple being perverted, and the
> innocent secretly wounded by their arrows, and to block that
> broad road which could be opened to the uncorrected commis-
> sion of sin, and for other just and reasonable motives known to
> Us; We therefore, having taken counsel of some of our Vener-
> able Brothers among the Cardinals of the Holy Roman Church,
> and also of Our own accord and with certain knowledge and
> mature deliberation, with the plenitude of the Apostolic power
> do hereby determine and have decreed that these same socie-
> ties, companies, assemblies, meetings, congregations or conven-
> ticles of Liberi Muratori or Francs Massons, or whatever name
> they may go by, are to be condemned and prohibited, and by
> Our present Constitution, valid for ever, We do condemn and
> prohibit them.[1]

Nearly one and a half centuries later Pope Leo XIII published an even fuller condemnation of freemasonry running
to over 8,000 words. In the intervening years a further twelve
papal condemnations of freemasonry had been published by
seven popes equally concerned at the undermining effect
that it was having on Christian belief. It is very clear that the
Vatican had been well aware of exactly what it was that it
found so abhorrent:

> For as soon as the constitution and the spirit of the Masonic sect
> were clearly discovered by manifest signs of its actions, by cases
> investigated, by the publication of its laws, and of its rites and
> commentaries, with the addition often of the personal testimony

of those who were in the secret, this Apostolic See denounced the sect of the Freemasons, and publicly declared its constitution, as contrary to law and right, to be pernicious no less to Christendom than to the State; We clearly saw and felt it to be Our duty to use Our authority to the very utmost against so vast an evil.[2]

Leo XIII was noted for being an extremely liberal pope, but he similarly saw the immense potential and real dangers of freemasonry:

. . . as all who offer themselves are received whatever may be their form of religion they thereby teach the great error of this age—that a regard for religion should he held as an indifferent matter, and that all religions are alike. This manner of reasoning is calculated to bring about the ruin of all forms of religion, and especially of the Catholic religion, which, as it is the only one that is true, cannot, without great injustice, be regarded as merely equal to other religions.[3]

He clearly saw that as the truth of the Christian faith was further undermined, there would ensue immense dangers to the whole structure of society, marriage, family life, civil obedience and education, with a resulting rise in communism!

It is now Our intention, following the example of Our predecessors, directly to treat of the Masonic Society itself, of its whole teaching, of its aims, and of its manner of thinking and acting in order to bring more and more into the light its power for evil, and to do what we can to arrest the contagion of this fatal plague. . . . As Our predecessors have many times repeated, let no man think that he may for any reason whatsoever join the Masonic sect; if he values his Catholic name and his eternal salvation as he ought to value them. Let no one be deceived by a pretence of honesty. It may seem to some that Freemasons demand nothing that is openly contrary to religion and morality . . . .[4]

The Grand Master of the Grand Lodge of France,

Dumesnil de Gramont, was in no doubt as to the severity of the Encyclical, and the significance of its source:

> What a terrible text this Encyclical contains, and one which our brothers ought to read frequently. Terrible and surprising too, when you consider that its author is still considered as the finest, the most clear-sighted and the most liberal of modern popes. One is overwhelmed at its vehement tones, the violent epithets, the audacity of the accusations, the perfidy of the appeals to secular repression . . . .[5]

Even though the Encyclical, in common with all papal condemnations, is most concerned with the spiritual threat caused by the deist, gnostic and rationalistic lure of freemasonry, it also reveals the methods of political and ecclesiastical influence which were evident in France and Italy.

Vicomte Leon de Poncins, in his widely researched book on the relationship between Rome and international freemasonry writes:

> It is perfectly obvious that Leo XIII was convinced of the extreme importance of the problem of Freemasonry for he referred to it on several occasions after Humanum Genus, in 1890, 1892, 1894 and in 1902. He published a double letter in 1892, one to the Archbishops and Bishops, and the other to the people of Italy, which was entirely concerned with the question of Freemasonry. In this letter he renewed and reinforced the themes he had elaborated in Humanum Genus.
>
> The letter began:
> 'The spirit common to all former sects which have revolted against Catholic institutions has sprung up with fresh vigour in that sect which is called Masonic. . . . Whole cities are overrun by its contagion: civil institutions are becoming more and more deeply penetrated with its inspiration. . . . Let us remember that Christianity and Freemasonry are fundamentally irreconcilable, so much so that to adhere to the one is to cut oneself off from the other.'[6]

De Poncins also quotes a later Encyclical, written on the

twenty-fifth anniversary of Leo's pontificate, which described freemasonry as seeking 'to exercise an occult overlordship upon society as we know it . . . .'

Following this, two Popes, Pius X (1906) and Pius XI (1937) came out against freemasonry.

Responses from the Supreme Congregation of the Holy Office in 1946 and 1949 are significant. The Italian archbishops had submitted questions concerning international freemasonry and were told:

> Scottish rite Masonry falls under the condemnation decreed by the Church against Masonry in general, and there is no reason to grant any discrimination in favour of this category of Masons. (1946)
>
> Since nothing has happened to cause any change in the decisions of the Holy See on this question, the provisions of Canon Law remain in full force for every kind of Masonry whatsoever. (April 20 1949)[6]

It could well be asked why, after more than two centuries of such consistently outspoken condemnation of freemasonry, a group within the Church were questioning whether certain parts of the craft could be considered outside the ban. This did not take place in a vacuum, but was part of a well-orchestrated international plan to make freemasonry respectable and gain acceptance for it, or at least for certain parts of it, within the Church of Rome. De Poncins considers that it had started in the 1920s, beginning very secretively but then becoming more public as writers published defences of the craft. Hopes for rapprochement between the Church and the craft were encouraged by the accession of Pope John XXIII and the liberalization of Roman Catholic attitudes:

> A sudden flowering of works devoted to Freemasonry blossomed forth from a variety of authors. Historians, philosophers, journalists, politicians and lecturers, all worked, each in his own

sphere, in favour of a reconciliation between the Catholic Church and Freemasonry.[7]

The main planks of their argument were as follows:

1. that the condemnations could not possibly be interpreted as being 'for ever' while there was the possibility of freemasonry changing its nature;
2. there had never been an open declaration of war between the craft and the Church;
3. that the motive for the condemnations was political, put forward in the guise of a religious issue.

Thus the argument gradually emerged that if certain parts of freemasonry could be shown to be not in opposition to the Church, then surely they ought to be recognized. De Poncins considers that the advocates of an agreement between Church and craft, particularly those within the Church, were advancing the following:

1. that the condemnations were, after all, a mistake and could not be justified. Indeed the Church could win respect by recognizing her error;
2. that the Vatican had never been able to formulate clearly and concisely valid motives for the condemnation;
3. that freemasonry is profoundly evolutionary, and from having been rationalist, agnostic and anti-Christian, it had become increasingly spiritual in its regular obediences. Therefore, the hostility with which the Church and freemasonry had opposed each other no longer had any meaning.

In its battle for acceptance by the Church of Rome, freemasonry in this country gained a very unexpected ally. Having read a book by Father J. A. Ferrer Benimeli *La Masoneria Despues del Concilio* (Masonry since the [Vatican] Council) in preparation for a lecture on 'Freemasonry of the

Future' to be given in February 1968 to the London Grand Rank Association (a body of experienced freemasons, all Past Masters of at least five years' standing), Harry Carr, a very senior mason, became an ardent advocate of a new understanding between Church and craft. When he gave his lecture he spoke at some length of the hope of bridging the gulf that had so long separated the craft from the Church of Rome. Clearly his dream was momentarily shattered when in the subsequent questiontime he was asked how he could possibly hope for this when the bookstall in Westminster Cathedral sold anti-masonic pamphlets. As a result, considering the pamphlets excessive, he wrote to the late Cardinal Heenan, and a meeting was arranged. Harry Carr states that the meeting was all that he could hope for—and more. The pamphlets were removed, but more significantly the Archbishop was sympathetic to Carr's distinction between English masonry and the atheistic or anti-Christian Grand Orient type, and promised to be 'an intermediary' to convince the authorities in Rome.

Carr records that nothing happened very quickly, in spite of rumours that the Vatican was going to revise its Code of Canon Law and in particular Canon 2335 relating to freemasonry and other secret societies. In April 1971 Cardinal Heenan and Carr met again and at that meeting the Archbishop told him about two pastoral cases where men, having been protestant masons, had married Catholic women, and were subsequently received into the Catholic faith on the authority of the Vatican without having to give up their masonry:

> His Eminence then showed me the letter from the Holy Office; it requested that no undue publicity should be given to it 'for fear of creating misunderstanding'.[8]

Carr states that he included this story by kind permission of Cardinal Heenan!

Opinion within the Church of Rome seemed to be changing. Mellor lists any number of masons and churchmen from many realms of international freemasonry who were involved in seeking to bring in this change of policy. After the apparent change of heart in the corridors of power in Rome, Carr states:

> There must be hundreds of dedicated Masons all over the world who have played some part in the achievement of this long desired end.[9]

The temporary relaxation came in 1974 and proved to be an astonishing and embarrassing exercise for the Church of Rome. In July of that year Cardinal Heenan received a communication from the Holy See which included the following:

> The Sacred Congregation for the Doctrine of the Faith . . . has ruled that Canon 2335 no longer automatically bars a Catholic from membership of masonic groups. . . . And so a Catholic who joins the Freemasons is excommunicated only if the policy and actions of the Freemasons in his area are known to be hostile to the Church.[10]

Following nearly two hundred and fifty years of clear, outright condemnation of all forms of freemasonry, this was an amazing about-face—Rome had relented under the weight of international pressure. What was even more remarkable was the timing, since it coincided with the beginning of official talks between the Catholic Church and German freemasons, under the joint direction of the German Bishops' Conference and the United Grand Lodges of Germany.

Six years' dialogue ensued and the report states that the meetings were held 'in an atmosphere of openness and objectivity'. The German masons were most co-operative, showing the bishops their complete craft rituals and other documents. The report gives details of a long and careful examination, but the conclusions which were reached only served to emphasize the truth of the traditional position and understanding. The report states that at the outset the bishops had been encouraged by several factors to consider that fundamental changes had taken place in German free-masonry, which could make it acceptable to the church, even though the craft in Germany had not previously been re-nowned for its anti-clericalism. Not the least of the reasons was that German freemasonry had been reduced by National-Socialist persecution to a quarter of what it had been! The Conference looked into the whole question of masonic encouragement of humanitarianism and human rights, good works, symbols and rites and anti-materialism. This followed discussion between the German Evangelical Church and the craft on the first degree. However, both they, and the German bishops, came up against basic and insurmountable obstacles. The bishops concluded: 'Belong-ing to it puts all the foundations of Christian life in ques-tion.'[11]

They put forward the following objections:

1. The masonic philosophical outlook, whilst containing strong humanitarian and ethical belief, encourages personal interpretation within a very wide area. Such subjectivism cannot be squared with faith in the re-vealed word of God interpreted within the Church's doctrinal congregation.
2. The masonic rejection of all dogma is incompatible with the Church's concept of truth by way of natural or revealed theology.
3. The masonic understanding is that all religions are equally important, no one religion having access to absolute truth. Masons hold that all faiths are, in effect, competing partners in pointing to God's truth. This implies a view of religion which is at odds with the basic Christian conviction about Christ's exclusive claims.
4. The masonic concept of God as 'the Great Architect of

the Universe' removes all sense of a God who speaks as Father and Lord. Their god is essentially deist—neutral, undefined and open to any interpretation.

5. The masonic vision of God does not allow us in any way to think of a God who reveals himself, again a basic Christian tenet.

6. Masonic toleration undermines the faith of a Catholic and his acknowledgement of the Church's teaching authority.

7. The masonic ritual contained in the three basic craft degrees resembles a sacramental ceremony in both word and symbol. It would appear that a man who has gone through these rites believes he has undergone an objective transformation.

8. The evidence of the rituals shows that ultimately freemasonry is concerned with ethical and spiritual perfection, and that there is no need for the grace of God, and for justification by faith in Christ. Baptism, confession and the eucharist are rendered useless if, as stated in the rituals, enlightenment and victory over death are attainable through the rituals themselves.

9. Masonic spirituality claims to cover life and death and requires total allegiance. This particular demand is totally incompatible with Catholic belief since it alone has the right to demand such faith and allegiance.

10. In some countries as much as 50% of the ritual degrees are known as 'Christian', and are allegedly only open to Christians. However, since this is only seen as a possible alternative to the masonic philosophy, parts of which are purely atheistic, in France for example, the two cannot harmonize.

11. It makes no difference whether lodges are friendly, neutral or hostile to the Church—insuperable difficulties still exist, as the above points show.

12. The discussions between German freemasons and the

evangelical churches revealed problems of reconciling the Christian doctrine of justification by grace with the first craft degree. Since discussions were limited to this degree the churches left the question of simultaneous membership to the individual.

The conclusion reached in the report was that masonry has changed—little at all!

> The contradictions which have been pointed out shake the very foundations of Christian existence. The examination in depth of the rituals and the ideal world of the Masons make it clear that it is impossible to belong to the Catholic Church and to Free-masonry at the same time.[12]

This thorough and open report left the Vatican in a most embarrassing position. Within a year they had gone some way towards returning to the traditional position. The declaration published by the Sacred Congregation for the Doctrine of the Faith blamed the fact that a private letter sent on July 19 1974 to some Episcopal Conferences had been made public, giving rise to 'erroneous and tendentious interpretations'. It stated that canonical discipline was still in force, without any modification, that excommunication and other penalties were still operative and that individual cases should be submitted to the judgement of ordinaries.

Any uncertainty which still remained was resolved by the statement issued on November 27 1983 in conjunction with the new code of Canon Law. This considered masons to be in a state of 'serious sin' and 'barred from the Eucharist'. It removed any power from bishops to give permission to Catholics of their diocese to join freemasonry.[13]

I have felt it important to include a fairly substantial history of the relationship between the Church of Rome and freemasonry because it shows us several important factors:

1. that since the early eighteenth century freemasonry has

changed little in character;

2. that it has always been possible to gain a fairly accurate picture of what goes on behind lodge doors;

3. that the Roman Church has persistently and consistently stood out against the influence and inherent belief contained within the craft and its competitive stance with the Church;

4. the increased pressure, internationally orchestrated by masons, to seek to win acceptance by the Church;

5. the importance of the support of the Church to freemasonry, many having spent much time in seeking to unite the two;

6. the real threat posed by the masonic beliefs and assumptions inherent in the craft rituals.

The Roman Catholic Church believes that its doctrines are incompatible with international freemasonry, both regular and Orient.

5

Other Churches' investigations

Methodist

'Methodist report urges resignation of masons and lodge
meetings' ban'—was the headline in a *Times* article on June
13th 1985. The Church's Faith and Order Committee had
spent nearly a year investigating the craft, its rituals and its
relationship with the Church. Their recommendations received wide coverage in the national press and caused much
consternation in Grand Lodge. The Methodists found themselves in an unfamiliar situation as the television companies
began pressing to broadcast their annual conference. What
had been for many years a relatively unnoticed gathering
suddenly became the focus of attention.

What is strange about this furore is that it was no sudden
new departure for Methodism. Nearly sixty years before, a
Methodist minister, the Rev. C. Penney Hunt, published a
book which caused the Wesleyan Conference to take
decisive action. Using only official and well-attested masonic
material, Penney Hunt had undertaken a very carefully researched work into what he saw as a 'menace, which if not

checked, may imperil the very existence of the Church. . . .'[1]
His book was considered by a number of Committees and
resulted in much debate at the 1927 Conference. The outcome was a unanimous acceptance of three resolutions by
the 600 members, of whom as many as a quarter were
masons:

1. 'Conference . . . recognises that Freemasonry, in its
   ritual and official language, is of a purely Theistic
   nature . . . and . . . the distinctive faith of Christianity
   can find no expression in its formulae, and that the
   Christian message of salvation, through faith in Christ,
   as the basis alike for home and foreign evangelisation is
   wholly incompatible with the claims which have often
   been put forward by Freemasons, both in writing and in
   speech.
2. An instruction to any ministers, seeing fit to join the
   craft 'to devote special care to maintaining the faith
   once delivered to the saints'.
3. 'The Conference is of the opinion that the holding of
   Masonic services on Methodist premises is highly in-
   expedient, but directs that whenever requests are received for such, the following safeguards must be
   complied with:
   (i) the consent of the superintendent, who shall be
        responsible for the programme of the service,
        which must be submitted to him;
   (ii) such services must be of a truly Christian charac-
        ter; must not be used for the advocacy of Free-
        masonry; and in prayers and hymns there must not
        be, by deletion or otherwise, a denial of the name
        of Christ as Saviour and Lord.'[2]

In spite of some subsequent furious activity by a few
masonic clergy in Methodism, no change was made and until
1981 nothing happened. It was at that time that these stand-

ing orders were left out, rather hastily overlooked by the conference of that year, who considered them to be covered by other standing orders. The Cornwall Synod moved these resolutions at their May 1984 meeting and this gave rise to the national investigation.

Grand Lodge, obviously keen to try to obtain an ally—and no doubt concerned about the return to the traditional position in the Church of Rome, and the current disquiet in both the Church of England and society in general—gave the Faith and Order Committee considerable help, even to the extent of submitting a completely revised text of the draft report!

The Faith and Order Committee report shows that they got right to the heart of craft freemasonry, having full texts of the rituals (Section 5). They recognized the high morality, charity, tolerance and respect within the craft (Sections 6 and 7). However, they condemned the practice of discussion and decision-making of Church business at Lodge meetings (Section 11), recognizing that masonic secrecy was not reasonably justified (Section 12). With regard to masonic oaths, there was distinct unease, they 'should never contain extravagant words just to add colour, nor should they refer to penalties which cannot be enforced' (Section 13). There was unease, too, about the practice of swearing secrecy prior to knowledge of the object of that secrecy—this could not be commended (Section 14). They warned against the danger of masonic commitment taking precedent over commitment to Christ, thereby making membership of the Methodist Church unacceptable, and were concerned about masonic prayer which expressly excluded Christ (Sections 15 and 16). Grave reservations were expressed over the 'secret knowledge' of the craft:

> The suggestion of secret knowledge becomes stronger as one proceeds through the degrees of the society and becomes explicit in the exaltation rites for the Royal Arch degree. . . . The

references to these secrets carry clear implications of a secret knowledge whose possession helps one to obtain immortal life, but there is no explicit reference to salvation and no claim that this is the only way to immortality. . . . (Section 18)[3]

In Section 19 mention is made of masonic rituals which would seem to be the equivalent of essential parts of Christian faith—death to life, darkness to light and the assumption, which is implicit in the ritual, that these are more than physical.

The most serious objection is cited in Section 20 of the report. It concerns the name given to the Supreme Being in the Royal Arch ritual—JAH-BUL-ON:

It has been suggested to us that this word is a description of God, but the ritual refers to the word as the name of God . . . it is clear that each of the three syllables is intended to be the name of a divinity in a particular religion. The whole word is thus an example of syncretism, an attempt to unite different religions in one, which Christians cannot accept.[3]

The report goes on:

Although Freemasonry claims not to be a religion or a religious movement, its rituals contain religious practices and carry religious overtones. It is clear that Freemasonry may compete strongly with Christianity. There is a great danger that the Christian who becomes a Freemason will find himself compromising his Christian beliefs or his allegiance to Christ, perhaps without realising what he is doing. Consequently our guidance to the Methodist people is that Methodists should not become Freemasons. (Sections 21/22)[3]

The committee probably went as far as they could in denouncing freemasonry without actually forbidding Methodists from joining. They asked all Methodists who were masons to consider these findings carefully and proposed standing orders forbidding masonic lodges or other meetings taking place on Methodist premises, proscribing services exclusively for masons, and giving guidelines on services that masons may have, subject to the permission of local Trustees.

The ensuing Conference debate in 1985 was a lively affair with speakers representing both sides. An amendment merely to receive the Report and to request comments from circuits and Synods with a final decision being made in 1987 was lost with only about thirty of the six hundred or so present voting in favour. The final resolution to accept the report and the standing orders was overwhelmingly adopted with again only about thirty against. Grand Lodge was apparently 'very sad' that the report followed a 'brief' investigation, and considered that 'any Methodist who has studied the report with a critical but open mind, will detect its flaws . . . .'[4] Clearly, more than five hundred Methodists would appear to the Grand Secretary of Grand Lodge not to have gone into this with open minds! A resolution three months later at a private meeting of more than thirty Methodist masons launched, by seventeen votes to three, an 'Association of Methodist Masons'—subject to the approval of the Grand Master and Grand Secretary!

Clearly, there was much concern within the Methodist Church at the pastoral pain that had been caused to many genuine and loyal Methodists. However, it is abundantly clear that the Methodist Church considered it vital to grasp this nettle and to seek to make the issues plain. What is remarkable is that their conclusions, after a thorough investigation which took no recognition of the German Catholic Bishops' Report, nor indeed of Penney Hunt's conclusions sixty years before, came to almost identical conclusions on the basic incompatibility of Christianity and freemasonry!

Other Churches

The conclusions of the Methodist Church continue the pattern established during the course of church history with regard to freemasonry. Walton Hannah wrote: 'No Church that has seriously investigated the religious teachings and implications of Freemasonry has failed to condemn it.'[5]

Earlier this century General Bramwell Booth felt so strongly about this that he sent a letter to every Salvation Army officer. He was concerned at the omission of Christ's name in the rituals:

> No language of mine could be too strong in condemning any Officer's affiliation which shuts Him outside its Temples; and which in its religious ceremonies gives neither Him nor His Name any place. . . . The place where Jesus Christ is not allowed is no place for any Salvation Army Officer. As for the future, the Army's views upon this matter will be made known to all who wish to become Officers, and acceptance of these views will be necessary before candidates can be received for training, and further, from this time it will be contrary for any Officer to join such a Society.[6]

In practice this has meant that men in training for leadership within the Salvation Army have been required to give a verbal assurance prior to acceptance for officership, and a written undertaking when beginning as a cadet, that they relinquish any attachment to a secret society. I gather that the only secret society that the Army has in mind is freemasonry.

A similar ruling had been made by the Reformed Presbyterian Church of Ireland, who made it a condition of membership that men abstain from affiliation to freemasonry. This was followed by a similar ruling in 1927 by the Free Presbyterian Church of Scotland.

In 1933 an independent commission of four bishops, the theological faculty of the University of Athens and a professor, reported back on freemasonry to the Bishops' Conference of the Church of Greece. Their conclusions were unanimous. In the rituals they saw unmistakable links with ancient Greek and Egyptian mysteries. They believed it to be a 'mystery-religion, quite different, separate and alien to the Christian faith', and considered it to undermine the Christian faith, exalting knowledge above faith.

> Thus, the incompatible contradiction between Christianity and Freemasonry is quite clear. It is natural that various Churches of other denominations have taken a stand against Freemasonry. Not only has the Western Church branded for its own reasons the masonic movement by numerous Papal encyclicals, but Lutheran, Methodist and Presbyterian communities have also declared it to be incompatible with Christianity. Much more has the Orthodox Catholic Church, maintaining in its integrity the treasure of Christian faith, proclaimed against it every time that the question of Freemasonry has been raised. Recently the Interorthodox Commission which met on Mount Aulos and in which representatives of all the Autocephalous Orthodox Churches took part, has characterised Freemasonry as a false and anti-Christian system.[7]

The practicalities of this were spelt out by the President, His Grace Archbishop Chrysostom of Athens: clergy would not be permitted to join the craft, and 'all the faithful children of the Church must stand apart from Freemasonry'. This, he said, was declared 'unanimously and with one voice'. I understand that in the last few years the Greek Orthodox church has reaffirmed this ban, but I have not been able to obtain a copy. More details of the stand taken by these and other churches, in particular the Lutheran Church, can be found in the tenth chapter of Walton Hannah's book, *Darkness Visible*. At the present time there is a great deal of interest in this subject in Sweden and Norway, where the state churches are Lutheran. In the former, membership is not secret and several bishops belong to what is claimed to be a Christian organization. Grand Lodge of England admits that its fellow lodges in Scandinavia are entirely for Christians; it recognizes but does not agree with their policy. In spite of this there is in Sweden such widespread concern about whether a pastor can serve both Church and lodge, that a Swedish court is having to decide! I can imagine St Paul despairing (1 Corinthians 6:1-6).

In Norway, there has recently been a growing concern about Christian involvement in the craft. This has been fuelled by a series of articles on the subject in Norway's leading Christian newspaper *Vart Land.* The debate is still continuing but the presiding Bishop of Oslo has expressed his views publicly in an interview with the newspaper, stating that although each individual's conscience must ultimately decide, he believes it best that clergymen should not be free-masons, citing exclusivity, secrecy, and dogmatic differences as the main problem areas.

In Britain the Baptist Union and some smaller churches have awaited decisions by the Methodist and Anglican Church before holding enquiries themselves.

Other churches within the Anglican communion are con-sidering taking action. This accords with moves outside the church in the police, local government, prison service, teach-ing profession, Liberal Party and national union of public employees to investigate, or issue warnings against, masonic membership.

For the churches though, the position is well summed up by the late John Wesley: 'Unite on the one Essential and allow individual liberty on secondary matters.' The masonic response would seem to be: 'Unite on the basis of the ele-ment common to every religion, and cut out the Christian essential.'

6

The Church of England

It is perhaps surprising that with the persistent condemnation of freemasonry by the Church of Rome for more than
two hundred years, and the enquiry and decision of the
Methodist Conference in 1927 that the problem of compatibility does not appear to have been raised within the Church
of England until 1951. There may be any number of reasons
for this—the predominance of liberalism within the Church,
the close association of establishment and freemasonry or
the fact that non-masons within the Church knew very little
about the craft.

It is interesting to see how freemasonry viewed it:

It would be fairly safe conjecture to assume that the great majority of English freemasons belong to the Church of England,
whether as merely 'C of E' (as the Army recruit who does not
claim to belong to any 'fancy religion' is conveniently labelled)
or as ardent adherents. The late Lord Fisher of Lambeth, Archbishop of Canterbury from 1945 to 1961, was Grand Chaplain in
1937 and 1939 while there are numerous devout priests who
serve as Chaplains of Grand Lodges and lodges. It came, therefore as something of a shock when an attack was launched on

the Order by a group of Anglican parsons.

The trouble started with an article in *Theology* . . . in January 1951; it was entitled 'Should a Christian be a Freemason?' and was from the pen of the Rev. Walton Hannah. . . .[1]

Walton Hannah, a Sussex clergyman, had been approached informally by a fellow cleric to join freemasonry. His reluctance to join anything about which he could know little in advance was met with surprise. Surely, he was told, if bishops could join, then it should be good enough for him! Hannah was not satisfied with this argument and determined to find out about the organization. He became most concerned at what he was discovering and wrote to his bishop for guidance.

The reply was more taken up with surprise tinged with indignation that I had discovered supposed secrets than with any anxiety to allay my misgivings. He said very courteously that if I did not like Freemasonry I had better not join, but he was not allowed to discuss these things with any who were not Masons. To which I wrote in return that I was truly appalled at the implications of this remark. I had made a prima facie case (and I then claimed no more) for the Craft being incompatible with Christianity, and appealed to a bishop for guidance. And his reply that he was bound by oath not to refute or even discuss such matters, although they admittedly concerned faith and morals, with any who were not similarly oath-bound to secrecy clearly implied that his Masonic obligation took precedence over his Episcopal oath to banish strange and erroneous doctrine. But there was no reply.[2]

Hannah decided to bring this concern into the public arena of the Church since he could not get answers to his questions from several bishops he contacted. His eight-page article in *Theology* magazine spoke about gnosticism and secrecy in general and masonry in particular. It was unemotional, setting out facts, quoting ritual, stating the position of the Roman Catholic and Methodist Churches and finishing with one question: Is the Church of England too mortally involved with this heresy to speak her mind?

Furious and emotive correspondence ensued and the matter was duly raised in the Church's governing body. To say that the debate was a set-up job would be something of an understatement. Bishop Mervyn Stockwood writing in the *Church of England Newspaper* explained:

> Some years ago there was a debate in Church Assembly when, so I am told by an Episcopal Mason who was present at it, the matter was laughed out of court and Cyril Garbett exploded the thing with first class ridicule![3]

A motion had been tabled by the Rev. R. Creed Meredith, son of Sir James Creed Meredith, Deputy Grand Master of Ireland from 1897 to 1911. The motion was that a commission be appointed to report on Hannah's article. Meredith, himself a mason, defended the craft, explaining, as he saw it, the aims and objects, and claimed that Hannah's attack had given pain and distress to hundreds of loyal churchmen throughout the country. It all seemed very plausible. However, right from the start at least one member of the Assembly was disturbed at the way this item was being stage-managed. On a point of order Mr W. H. Saumarez-Smith (Salisbury) questioned whether matters of theology or doctrine came within the purview of the Assembly under its constitution. He could not see how the motion could be adequately discussed without going into theological enquiry, but the Chairman dismissed the request, stating that the motion was merely to do with appointing a Commission which would report back to the Assembly about whether the House of Bishops should be asked to consider any theological question arising from Hannah's article.

Meredith was followed by a succession of masonic members, who virtually monopolized the debate. The Archbishop of York (not a mason) spoke in a highly contemptuous manner of the concerns raised.

Masonic historians, Pick and Knight, note the significance and importance of his intervention.

> Doctor Garbett then asked whom would the proposed Commission reassure? 'I am reassured (turning to Archbishop Fisher of Canterbury, who was presiding) by your Grace's being a member of the Order and by the fact that a distinguished layman, Lord Scarborough, is Grand Master of the Order.'
>
> The Assembly then rejected the motion with only one dissentient, a result which the mover explained he welcomed and had hoped for.[4]

Another masonic historian records that it 'was firmly handled and came to nothing. It was, however, clearly desirable that the opponents of Freemasonry should be given the least possible opportunity for attack.'[5] It was clear that masons within the Church organized themselves very well in order to divert debate. The real theological issues were totally overlooked by the defence, who appealed to sentimentality, episcopal involvement and social standing. The normally conservative *Church Times* was not impressed, however. In an editorial, it referred to

> the patent manoeuvres behind the scenes by which discussion has been stifled in Convocation and side-tracked in the Assembly. . . . There is a sheer lack of logic in saying: 'We have nothing to fear from enquiry. Therefore there must on no account be an enquiry.'[6]

At the close of the debate a point of order was raised as to the precedent set in 'members putting down motions, when from the outset they intended to achieve the exact contrary to the motions which they put down'. The masonic archbishop chairing the session considered it 'fair . . . in this case'! Hannah's prima facie case and genuine concerns remained unanswered. The widely held view that the Church of England was largely run by masons, was somewhat reinforced by this debate.

Bishop Stockwood cites in his autobiography three unfortunate incidents involving freemasonry, one of which was a request for a funeral service in which the words 'Jesus Christ' were omitted from the prayers and the word 'Architect' inserted. Also, the cross was to be removed from the altar. He refused permission and 'stirred up a hornet's nest'. When he took issue on another masonic problem, he seriously strained a close friendship with Archbishop Fisher who chastened him for not consulting fellow bishops over this particular matter, accusing him of arrogance.

> Some of my contemporaries at Cambridge openly told me they had signed on in order to climb the preferment ladder. In particular it was a pity, it seemed to me, that there should be a division among the bishops. We were supposed to be a brotherhood but here was a secret society within the brotherhood. . . . In fact I had consulted the Archbishop of Canterbury who warmly supported me in the action I had taken. I sent a copy of the Archbishop's letter to his predecessor. Alas, it strained our relationship to breaking point. I was sad because Geoffrey Fisher had been a good friend and adviser. Moreover, during my first year at Southwark, when I had no home of my own, I had lived at Lambeth Palace for several months and became very fond of the Archbishop and his wife. What grieved me especially was the fact that it was the Masonic issue that led to the point of no return. It more than confirmed my view that it was unhelpful for some bishops to belong to a secret society which demanded an absolute loyalty. It was calculated to divide us into two groups and could lead to conflict.[7]

When I spoke to Bishop Stockwood he confirmed that the great majority of bishops under Geoffrey Fisher were masons. When he arrived in the Southwark Diocese he found that each suffragan, and archdeacon was a mason. He confirmed that today scarcely any bishops are masons, merely 'a few suffragans who see their main chance of making diocesan bishop by being a member of the Lodge'!

In 1962 Bishop Stockwood had called for a 'considered opinion' from Convocation, believing it to be a serious matter, doing the Church's image no good at all. He was clearly at a loss to understand how 'any man who treats his faith seriously . . . need . . . take up membership in a secondary religious organisation.'[8] The call went unheeded. But he was not alone in his concern.

The initial reaction of Dr E. L. Mascall of Christ Church, Oxford was to decline an invitation to write a foreword to Hannah's second book, but as he looked at the evidence he became increasingly concerned about how 'many devout Christians manage by some obscure mental process to be freemasons',[9] and about the deliberate attempt to prevent investigation of the matter.

Hannah's first book *Darkness Visible* which dealt with the basic theological objections to freemasonry, with particular reference to the craft degrees and the Holy Royal Arch, had a very far-reaching impact. Its greatest value was that it gave a clear statement of the issues and concerns, and exploded the myth that freemasonry had to remain secret. The rituals are quoted in full, and go some way to explaining local variations. The book has gone into fourteen editions and is still a substantial seller. It is even carried by the largest masonic publisher and is used by many masons as a way of facilitating the learning of their ritual! Needless to say, its accuracy has never been seriously challenged, but often confirmed!

Christian by Degrees was a companion volume, which was written in order to examine the validity of the claims made by some within the Anglican Church that there were many masonic orders which were Christian. The book destroyed this myth completely. Hannah, in fact, had become increasingly disenchanted with the Church of England and resigned in 1955 in order to enter the Roman Catholic Church. He trained as a priest at Rome and was posted to Montreal,

Canada, where he died in 1966. Within three days of his death, the writer of *Light Invisible,* a book which sought to answer criticism of Hannah's first book, also died. Writing anonymously under the pseudonym 'Vindex', this Anglican vicar, who was in fact a fellow cleric in Sussex, had unsuccessfully sought to do battle with Hannah. His arguments, at first acclaimed by masonic reviews, were later disowned when it was seen that they did the craft more harm than good.

One of the reviewers of Hannah's work, Dr D. R. Denman, a former mason himself, makes some interesting and illuminating comments about Hannah's work:

> My experience enables me to appraise his book and to claim it as in every way worthy. The conclusion he arrives at is unassailable; Christ and the Craft are fundamentally opposed to each other.

He continues:

> Well I remember the wave of nausea as I stood an initiate outside the Masonic Lodge and heard myself referred to as a poor candidate in a state of darkness who by God's help was seeking the light. God's grace had already shone in my heart to give the light of the knowledge of the glory of God in the face of Jesus Christ: this I knew, and as I stood there listening to the first utterance of Masonic ritual I was aware of rampant evil. In vain I sought for some acknowledgement of the Light of the World in the worship and ritual of the degrees that followed. There was nothing. The sense of blasphemy had become, by the middle of the Third Degree ceremony, so overwhelming that I was moved to protest and to leave the Temple—never to return.[10]

Superficially it may seem that nothing much happened within the Church over the twenty-five years that followed the Assembly's consideration (or lack of it) of freemasonry. There were occasional sermons and tracts, some local agitation, but no real action. However, if the Provincial and Grand Year Books of the Craft over this period are examined, substantial changes can be observed. Very few clergy appear to have joined and senior chaplaincy posts are increasingly taken by less senior churchmen. A survey of nearly 150 bishops, suffragans and assistant bishops revealed that less than half a dozen admitted membership while more than half clearly saw that conflict would arise if someone were both a freemason and a minister. Many spoke with a good understanding of the problems, often the result of first hand experience. Many said that they would have nothing to do with masonic services in church which they clearly saw as compromising the Christian faith.[11]

The question of the relationship of Church and craft came up in a slightly obsure way at the February 1976 session of General Synod. Dr Barbara Cawthorne, lay member for Lichfield, attacked the sale of church buildings for use as masonic halls. Her conclusion from personal counsel, that freemasonry was anti-Christian brought a response from a large proportion of those present: 'Dr Cawthorne's brief speech brought considerable applause from synod members.'[12]

Three years later controversy broke out at Durham Cathedral when objections were raised against the acting Dean, by correspondents to the *Church Times*, about masons taking part in Evensong dressed in their regalia. (Incidentally, this is strictly against the instruction given by Grand Lodge that regalia should be worn in public only in exceptional circumstances.) The masonic Dean of Gloucester preached at the service. It was, however, statements made by the acting Dean of Durham which sparked off considerable correspondence. His attack on the theological students who instigated the objections and his defence of masons as being 'wholly good in their good works' seemed a strange position for a Christian to take. His use of the word 'good' was clearly at odds with that of his Master (Luke 18:18-19).

Pastoral situations such as this had often been previously swept under the carpet by Church authorities but now, in the general climate of unease about freemasonry, more people were prepared to speak out. Stephen Knight refers to a tragic pastoral situation into which I had been called, where a local incumbent, within a very short time of his arrival in the parish, fell foul of the local masons. His very reasonable requests for assurances about the nature of a proposed service to be held in his church met with a hastily-called emergency meeting of the Church Council, who demanded his apology or their mass resignation. Yet he had merely followed his bishop's advice! The damage this did to both him and his family was not short-lived. It left a nasty taste and a deep scar. Several unconnected pastoral breakdowns have occurred in one diocese in the west country—with some very inconsistent decisions by the Bishop. It seems that the prime consideration in each one has been the status of masons involved, regardless of the moral and spiritual implications!

Situations like this are fortunately fairly uncommon but the growing awareness of the spiritual compromises involved in belonging to masonry was reflected in the February 1984 General Synod, when the Chairman of the Doctrine Commission was questioned about the compatibility of the craft with Christianity. It was widely felt by those 'in the know' in Synod that this was not the best way to approach the question, and the Bishop of Winchester's unhelpful and somewhat dismissive remarks did nothing to allay the concern.

A year later, at the February 1985 session, Mr R. E. C. Clark (Lincoln) moved a motion to 'bring forward for debate a report which considers the compatibility or otherwise of Freemasonry with Christianity'. Mr Clark spoke from a position of professed ignorance about the craft, though from what he said, it would seem that his little knowledge was at least very accurate. Four other contributions to the debate were made, two against an inquiry (from masonic supporters) and two in favour. The overwhelming vote reflected a very clear desire to look into the question of freemasonry's compatibility with Christianity.

At the February 1986 session of General Synod the seven names of the Commission members were published, two of them being masons—the Dean of St Albans and Dr Robert Hart (Exeter). Questions had been addressed to the Archbishop of Canterbury, at the July 1985 session about the composition of this group and assurances were given that it would not be chaired by a mason and that any non-mason member would not be the wife or a close relative of someone in the craft.

The report of this group, which is due to be finished by the end of 1986, is eagerly awaited. It is to be hoped that they will be allowed to consider the real issues rather than be side-tracked by the familiar assurances of the craft's basic morality and traditional reputation, which few would dispute.

7
The craft degrees—
the mainstream of freemasonry

Whether he be monarch or machine minder, a man must enter freemasonry through the craft degrees. Before a man can start to go through the plethora of higher degrees, he must first be initiated, passed and raised through the three craft degrees which are conferred in the approximately 7,500 London and local provincial lodges scattered throughout England and Wales. I expect that most of us have seen local masonic lodges from time to time in the heart of our larger towns and cities. Often resembling a church building, or so it would seem from the outside, they are the meeting places for masons. Each individual lodge does not normally have its own building. It is usual for many lodges to share rooms in one building, so, for example, in a city such as Leicester, forty lodges use one building in the centre of the city at different times for their meetings.

It is claimed that any male over the age of twenty-one can join a lodge, and thus, in theory, it is possible to walk into any lodge in the country and ask to join. However, before a man can join he must first have a proposer and seconder and his name must be submitted to the committee of the particular lodge, who will subsequently interview him. This is to ascertain whether he is a suitable person, and whether attendance at masonic meetings and Lodge of Instruction would disrupt his domestic or business life in any way. Assuming that the committee are content, then the candidate's name is submitted at the next open lodge and his application decided by a show of hands or a ballot. Normally, it would take three dissidents to reject a candidate but local by-laws do in some cases make it one 'black-ball'.

Various hints were made to me over the years that it would be very good for me to join the lodge. Grand Lodge claims that the craft never invites anyone to join. However, this is not true in practice. I have interviewed men who have been asked to join, and who, in some cases, have even been made aware that the lodge had discussed their membership without their prior knowledge, well before they were approached. Appeals are also made in old boys' school magazines or journals. I was even invited to join by a clerical colleague whom I had met for the first time only a few minutes before, while strolling in the grounds of Canterbury Cathedral one sunny Sunday morning. He informed me that I would have no problem getting in as a friend of his would act as seconder and he knew his lodge would have no objections!

An accepted candidate will attend a Lodge of Instruction to prepare him for his initiation. He will be told little about the first degree and nothing about the actual ceremony. Again, this is the official line, but in practice candidates sometimes have a fair idea of what will happen. Most, however, have not the faintest idea of the content and significance of the religious ritual.

The candidate is informed of the date and time for his initiation. When he presents himself at the lodge he must remove his jacket or waistcoat, collar (if detachable) and tie. He must leave behind all metal items such as a watch, cuff-

links, money, keys etc. His shirt is unbuttoned to the waist to
bare his left breast, while his right sleeve only is rolled up
above the elbow. Similarly, his left trouser leg is rolled up
above the knee (whether it be his own trousers or a pair of
pyjama trousers) and he wears a slipper with an open back,
so as to be slipshod. He is blindfolded, and a noose is placed
around his neck with its end hanging down his back. Most of
these strange practices have symbolic significance. The candidate then waits in an ante-room adjacent to the lodge for
three knocks which are made from within by the Inner
Guard. These are returned by the Tyler who will have prepared him. They indicate that the lodge and candidate are
both ready ('properly tyled').

When it has been ascertained from inside the lodge that
none but masons are present, the lodge door is opened and
the Inner Guard asks who it is that the Tyler has with him.
The response describes the initiate as a 'poor Candidate in a
state of darkness . . . of his own free will and accord properly
prepared, humbly soliciting to be admitted to the mysteries
and privileges of Freemasonry'.[1] The Inner Guard informs
him that he will obtain these privileges 'by the help of God'.
The Worshipful Master then intervenes, confirming the
Inner Guard's assertion, by informing the candidate that he
is to kneel 'while the blessing of Heaven is invoked on our
proceedings'!

Thus right from the beginning of a man's initiation into
craft freemasonry, he is informed that God will be with him
to assist him in his quest to be freed from his state of darkness, and that God is willing to bless whatever he will be
taught in the rituals that are before him, and will teach him
masonic belief and practice. The symbolism reinforcing his
apparent status, poor and in darkness, demonstrated by the
blindfold and impoverished clothing, serves to confirm the
understanding that within freemasonry there is something
deeply spiritual to enrich the life of the person who admits

his need and submits to its practices. The prayer of the Worshipful Master asks that the candidate 'be enabled to unfold the beauties of true godliness' assisted by the 'secrets of our masonic art'. The Worshipful Master then seeks to ascertain whether the candidate believes in God, and when such faith is elicited a somewhat ambiguous statement is made:

> Right glad am I to find your faith so well founded: relying on such sure support you may safely rise and follow your leader with a firm but humble confidence, for where the name of God is invoked, we trust no danger can ensue.

If by the words 'follow your leader' the ritual is referring to the Junior Deacon, the candidate has no idea who his leader is. If, however, the reference is to God, then again the implication is that in some way God will lead the initiate on through masonry. The former reference seems more likely as the Junior Deacon then leads the candidate, still blindfolded, around the lodge, in front of all the members. En route he is introduced to the Junior and Senior Warden in the same way as he was to the Inner Guard at his entrance. The candidate is then addressed by the Worshipful Master who seeks to ascertain that he is entering the craft 'unbiassed by the improper solicitation of friends against your own inclination, and uninfluenced by mercenary and other unworthy motive', and that he will serve the craft and his fellow-men well and continue to progress through the initiation. Further ritual by way of steps continues and the candidate stands in front of the Worshipful Master with the Senior and Junior Deacons by his side.

> It is my duty to inform you that Masonry is free, and requires a perfect freedom of inclination in every Candidate for its mysteries. It is founded on the purest principles of piety and virtue
> . . . .

So here we have it! The assurance that freemasonry is based on sublime religious virtues, and the inference that it is unequalled elsewhere. The Master continues:

> . . . it possesses great and invaluable privileges, and in order to secure those privileges to worthy men, and we trust to worthy men alone, vows of fidelity are required, but let me assure you that in those vows there is nothing incompatible with your civil, moral or religious duties. . . .

The statement that freemasonry contains the 'purest principles of piety and virtue' flatly contradicts the assurance that there is 'nothing incompatible with your . . . religious duties'. Jesus is the truth, that is his claim (John 14:6). Anyone who follows him knows that this virtue, let alone the purest expression of it, can be found in him alone. He is the complete revelation of God. St Paul wrote: 'In Him all the fulness of Deity dwells in bodily form, and in Him you have been made complete' (Colossians 2:9-10).

For someone born again of the Spirit of God, and filled with his Spirit there can be no place for anything or anyone claiming equal or higher revelation. There can be no higher knowledge of God nor practice of his will than through his Son. By its own credentials freemasonry stands condemned. There is an interesting Christian parallel between the Worshipful Master's speech and St Paul's second letter to Timothy: 'And the things which you have heard from me in the presence of many witnesses, these entrust to faithful men, who will be able to teach others also' (2 Timothy 2:2).

Assuming that the initiate is willing, he must next undertake a 'solemn obligation', in other words, swear an oath on the Bible never to reveal in any way the secrets or mysteries of the craft to a non-mason. This is made under a threat of barbaric punishment: that of his throat being cut and his tongue torn out! These penalties still prevail in freemasonry, in spite of some outcry against them. As a compromise, in 1964 permissible alternatives were sanctioned which speak of 'ever bearing in mind the traditional penalty . . .', but which in fact still have the effect of causing the candidate to appreciate that these rituals contain something deeply secretive which must not in any circumstances be revealed to, or even discussed with, those outside. This is far worse than the schoolboy pacts of secrecy which many of us engaged in because what is being demanded is a blanket assurance and commitment that everything learnt within the lodge will be kept secret, whether it be good or bad! Can any man, particularly a Christian, be reasonably asked to keep secret something that he has thus far been led to believe is to do with the highest form of social, moral and religious living? And if it is not, must he then not be permitted to share his concern with a non-mason whose opinion he may value and seek?

A few masons regard this oath, sworn on the Bible and sealed with a kiss, as almost worthless and freely talk about the rituals and ceremonies. The majority regard it as serious and binding. On several occasions I have spoken to men who have lived in fear of revealing masonic secrets though they have genuinely felt uneasy at the direction the knowledge was taking them. When they realized that I already knew what they were talking about, and they weren't betraying any secrets, the grave-clothes were loosened and with a sense of relief they settled down to talk with me.

The question of oaths is a difficult one for a Christian. Some genuinely believe that it is unchristian, preferring their 'yes' to be 'yes' and their 'no' to be 'no' (Matthew 5:34-37), while others will swear under oath if it is felt to be necessary, in a Court, for example. The particular point here is whether a masonic oath is necessary, and indeed valid. Several masons have told me that the real secret of freemasonry is 'the fellowship'. If this is true, and I suspect it is, then there is clearly no need to keep that secret! If the secrecy is to do with the passwords and rituals, then again it is unnecessary, since it is by no means difficult to purchase by mail order many different forms of masonic ritual and exposures of it.

Craft rituals vary greatly in their use of abbreviated forms. Each one is sold using many initials and abbreviations for key-words in order to mislead the uninformed but there has been no effort to standardize the system, and even within the same ritual words and phrases may appear by initials in one place and in full later on! In some parts of the world, rituals are available to outsiders and are not kept secret. This happened in Germany with the dialogue between the craft and the Roman Catholic bishops.

As to validity, it must be asked whether the oath of secrecy, whether bearing in mind or actually quoting murderous penalties, is serious or not. If it is serious, then it is illegal, since it is a murder pact. Moreover, it involves swearing on the Bible to do something which is contrary to God's will as revealed in the Bible. If it is not to be taken seriously, then it means that the name of God is taken in vain and so the third of the Ten Commandments is broken. If anyone feels bound by masonic secrecy I explain this to him. If he comes to believe that it was sinful to take such an oath, I simply ask him to confess it to God and renounce it, and to be free from it.

The ritual follows with what is in some ways a more effective punishment for disclosure:

> . . . of being branded as a wilfully perjured individual, void of all moral worth, and totally unfit to be received into this worshipful Lodge, or any other warranted Lodge, or society of men who prize honour and virtue above the external advantages of rank and fortune.

But a Christian has a far higher calling—that of sharing the truth that sets men free. We are called to expose darkness and any hold which the 'light' of freemasonry has on a man should be firmly resisted. Indeed the next stage in the ritual is a question from the Worshipful Master:

> Having been kept for a considerable time in a state of darkness,

69

what in your present situation, is the predominant wish of your heart?

The Junior Deacon prompts the candidate: 'Light.'
His blindfold is removed. He will now be able to see! The Worshipful Master continues:

> Having been restored to the blessing of material light, let me point out to your attention what we consider the three great, though emblematical lights of Freemasonry, they are the Volume of Sacred Law, the Square and the Compasses. The Sacred writings are to govern our faith, the Square to regulate our actions and the Compasses to keep us in due bounds with all mankind, particularly our brethren in Freemasonry.

Lodges are permitted to use any holy writings as their sacred volume, any or all! Harry Carr states that in Lodge Singapore (No. 7178) there are four different volumes on the pedestal at any one time, whilst in the Grand Lodge of Iran there are three versions in use (the Koran, the Zend Avesta and the King James Version of the Bible). Masonry thus holds that all volumes sacred to men are equally valid. This completely denies the unique authority claimed by the Bible and by Jesus as the Word of God. It is intrinsic to masonic belief that a higher revelation of God can be found, beyond that revealed by such sacred volumes and that there is a superior way of living, which only masonry allegedly imparts! This is why no one book is considered worthy of particular regard within the rituals. The Old Testament, as we shall see, is regarded as legend. Its stories are quarried to provide images and allegories that further masonic teaching.

It is then revealed to the candidate that he has escaped two threats of death by not rushing forward whilst blindfolded: the poniard and the cable-tow. These symbols of the power of death have been held respectively in front of and behind him as he moved towards the lodge. Thus, to have held back or to have rushed forward would have proved fatal! However, he is solemnly reminded that the greatest danger is still present—that of revealing such secrets as will be entrusted to him—the penalty being that of having his throat cut. The secrets of this first degree consist of a sign, a token and a word. The first degree sign is made by placing the right hand with the thumb extended in the form of a square to the left of the windpipe and drawing it smartly across the throat and dropping it to the side. The token or grip is also demonstrated by the Worshipful Master who adjusts the initiate's handshake to put distinct pressure of his thumb on the first joint of the hand. As the grip is exchanged the initiate is informed that this grip demands a word to accompany it and the word, which 'should never be given at length, but always by letters or syllables' is BOAZ. The candidate is informed by both the Master and the Junior Deacon that he must be most cautious about divulging it, for the word is derived from the left hand pillar of the porchway or entrance of King Solomon's Temple. It is named after the great grandfather of King David and it means 'in strength'.

The candidate is then walked round the lodge and examined for this knowledge of the three secrets of this degree by the Junior and Senior Wardens. He returns to the Worshipful Master who invests him with the distinguishing badge of a mason, an apron made of lambskin. I would suspect that it is no coincidence that the newly initiated mason is encouraged to put on the lamb. Jesus Christ, even hundreds of years before his birth, was called the Lamb of God, and was acclaimed as such by John the Baptist (John 1:29). John the Divine saw in the revelation those whose robes were made white in the blood of the Lamb (Revelation 7:14). The Senior Warden tells the newly initiated mason that this badge is:

> . . . more ancient than the Golden Fleece or Roman Eagle, more honourable than the Garter or any other Order in existence, being the badge of innocence and the bond of friendship.

This is a preposterous claim. Is a man being asked to reckon himself innocent before God? This is surely the only possible explanation of this religious ritual which is supposedly carried out with the blessing of God. Yet Christ alone is able to give us the badge of innocence before God, and that badge is his blood shed on the cross, his body broken for the world, to bring forgiveness and healing. St Paul advised the Christians in Corinth to beware since they were in the midst of rampant heresy: 'For such men are false apostles, deceitful workers, disguising themselves as apostles of Christ. And no wonder, for even Satan disguises himself as an angel of light' (2 Corinthians 11:13-14).

Masonic heresy may be more subtle but it is still very plain to see. However ancient the virtue, however honourable and commendable the works, a man cannot stand righteous before God without Christ.

This investiture is followed by an instruction from the Master which resembles that given by Christ in the Sermon on the Mount (Matthew 5:23-24):

> Let me add to the observations of the Senior Warden, that you are never to put on that badge should you be about to visit a Lodge in which there is a Brother with whom you are at variance, or against whom you entertain animosity. In such cases it is expected that you will invite him to withdraw in order amicably to settle your differences, which being happily effected, you may clothe yourselves. . . .

The ritual goes on to speak of circumstances when differences could not easily be resolved, advocating absence of one or both parties, 'rather than disturb the harmony of the Lodge'. We can see very plainly here what happens when you attempt a form of Christian teaching without Christ: it becomes a way of legalism more concerned for the system or the institution than for the individual. It was Christ's desire and command that there be no sham or pretence within his body the church. The supreme expression of that unity comes as we gather together around the Lord's Table to share in his communion meal as one body. It was the failure to recognize, or discern his body rightly that led to sin in the church at Corinth. In 1 Corinthians 11 St Paul spoke out against the abuse of this precious sacrament through divisions and factions. Our Lord is concerned for each individual (see, for example, Matthew 7:14, Ephesians 4:26). Each person must discover and live the full Christian life, set free from all hostility, resentment, jealousy and anger. Man was not created for hostility, but for peace, love and joy. As he is set free to be at one with his brothers, so he is able, by the grace of Jesus, to be at one with God: 'If someone says, "I love God," and hates his brother, he is a liar; for the one who does not love his brother whom he has seen, cannot love God whom he has not seen' (1 John 4:20).

We have already seen how freemasonry claims to express the most devout piety, but when we teach any ethical system, however high its morals (though here we see freemasonry is something far less than Christ's way), we retreat into the very system of legalism from which Christ sought to release us. It is only as his Spirit is allowed to invade a person's being that the old life can be overcome, and strength be found to defeat the ways of the world and the wiles of the devil.

The candidate, who is now effectively initiated, listens to a speech from the Worshipful Master about the masonic foundation which is Charity and 'has the approbation of Heaven and earth'. He is offered the opportunity to give to those in need, which of course he is unable to do since he has been divested of metal and valuables prior to entry. He is reminded that as he has been received into the craft, poor and penniless (though a little later he is told that he must pay the initiation fees!) so he must always remember to treat brother masons in need in the same way and give them charity.

The earlier reference to purity is taken up by the Worshipful Master in a further speech explaining the working tools of an Entered Apprentice freemason: the gauge, the common gavel and the chisel:

> . . . the twenty-four inch Gauge represents the twenty-four
> hours of the day, part to be spent in prayer to Almighty God,
> part in labour and refreshment, and part in serving a friend or
> Brother in time of need, without detriment to ourselves or
> connections. . . .

Throughout masonic ritual there is constant reference to
God and duty to him. The way of life under God encouraged
by masons is very good and laudable. There is no doubt of
that. It is in many ways 'the right way to live'. It appeals to
that part of us which has an appreciation of what is right and
wrong. It is easy for us to believe the lie that says to live
rightly in some way makes us acceptable to God. The explanation of the gavel takes this further:

> The common Gavel represents the force of conscience, which
> should keep down all vain and unbecoming thoughts which
> might obtrude during any of the aforementioned periods, so that
> our words and actions may ascend unpolluted to the Throne of
> Grace.

Isaiah, speaking as God's mouthpiece, merely stated that
this is impossible:

> For all of us have become like one who is unclean,
> And all our righteous deeds are like a filthy garment;
> And all of us wither like a leaf,
> And our iniquities like the wind, take us away.[2]

God sent Jesus into the world because no one at all is
righteous. Moreover we know that without faith it is impossible to please God. Our very best actions are tainted by
sin and there is nothing we can do about it. Sin has caused
separation between God and man and we cannot redeem
ourselves. Jesus Christ is the way, the only way (John 14:6).
He did not come primarily to show us how to live or to teach
us about morals. He demonstrated God's life by showing

74

that it means the death of self and resurrection to new life. Learning apparently new facts about God and how to live a better life will not in any way change the basic alienation between God and man. Neither freemasonry, nor any other life system, can make our thoughts and our actions 'unpolluted', acceptable and pleasing to God.

The Entered Apprentice is allowed to return to the anteroom to put on his normal clothes and on his arrival back in the lodge he is given the Worshipful Master's charge after initiation. He is congratulated on being admitted to the 'ancient and honourable institution' which has 'subsisted from time immemorial, no institution can boast a more solid foundation than that on which Freemasonry rests . . .'. He is reminded of the importance of 'serious contemplation of the Volume of Sacred Law' and informed that 'the important duties that you owe to God' will be taught in due course. The charge is full of moral, social and civil guidance and the newly initiated mason is ordered to abstain 'from every topic of political or religious discussion'. It concludes:

> From the very commendable attention you appear to have given this charge, I am led to hope you will duly appreciate the value of Freemasonry, and indelibly imprint on your heart the sacred dictates of truth, of Honour and of Virtue.

It can be seen that from start to finish in this, the first degree of craft freemasonry, with its frequent use of words such as sacred, true godliness, help of God, blessings, faith, truth, heaven, darkness and light, different names allegedly referring to God, together with religious trappings and terminology, processions, deacons, wardens, wands, hymns, prayers, and the emphasis on facing east, any man entering may well consider that he is on a path to fulfilling any religious duty or need. This direction continues through the other two craft degrees and into the Holy Royal Arch.

C. Penney Hunt, in his eminently researched *The Menacea*

of Freemasonry to the Christian Faith, commenting on some of the points I raise, writes: 'How can any Christian whose brain does not exist in water-tight compartments stand the first night of Freemasonry?'[3]

Fellow craft

Several masons have told me that this second craft degree came as something of an anti-climax, in many ways being very similar to the Entered Apprentice ritual, and lacking the heightened drama of the Master Mason degree. Rule 172 of the Book of Constitutions, given to each mason at his initiation states that:

> . . . no Lodge shall confer a degree on any Brother at a less interval than four weeks from his receiving the previous degree, and every ceremony performed in contravention of this provision shall be void.

This broad rule, with very rare exception, means that progress through the craft degrees is slightly controlled. Indeed it has been quite normal for men to wait months or even years before being 'passed' or 'raised'. Some more senior masons have been concerned at recent moves to push young aspiring masons quickly through the craft degrees, which seems to be the result of what is generally reckoned to be a growing shortage of men of calibre to take many of the leading positions in several parts of the country, particularly in the London area.

Before his 'passing' into this second degree, the candidate is questioned by the Worshipful Master in open lodge (with those who have only attained the Entered Apprentice degree being asked to leave). The candidate is asked: 'Where were you first prepared to be made a Mason?'

The response, prompted by the Junior Deacon, is, 'In my heart.'

76

Freemasonry obviously sees itself as something that must evolve from the deepest part of man—that which controls his body and, in spiritual terms, his belief. In one sense it could be construed as seeking to give a man a new heart, or at least a renewed one.

Jesus said: 'Where your treasure is, there will your heart be also' (Matthew 6:21).

St Paul emphasized the vital importance of what we believe in our heart: 'If you confess with your mouth Jesus as Lord, and believe in your heart that God raised Him from the dead, you shall be saved; for with the heart man believes, resulting in righteousness, and with the mouth he confesses, resulting in salvation' (Romans 10:9-10).

According to the ritual, this desire of the heart is given public expression in 'a convenient room adjoining the Lodge' where the candidate recounts his initiation: 'in the body of a Lodge, just, perfect and regular'. Prompted again by the Junior Deacon, he goes on to explain to his fellow lodge members that his initiation took place 'when the sun was at its meridian'. This strange paradox, since in all likelihood he was initiated in the evening, is explained by the fact that freemasonry, being universal, must always be under the place where the sun is shining at its brightest!

The Worshipful Master asks: 'What is freemasonry?'

The candidate must give what has generally been accepted to be the classic definition of freemasonry, namely: 'A peculiar system of morality, veiled in allegory and illustrated by symbols.'

It is interesting that freemasonry carefully steers clear of identifying itself as a religion when it is manifestly clear that the overriding impression from the craft degrees at least, is of something deeply religious. The allegory and symbols undeniably propound spiritual values. The Master questions the candidate further about his membership and then asks whether he is ready to undertake this degree of a fellow craft. Having given a further pledge of secrecy and caution, the candidate is shown the pass grip and password (Shib-boleth). This must be committed to memory, otherwise, he is told that he 'cannot gain admission into a Lodge in a superior degree'.

Assuming that the degree is to be conferred, the lodge is then officially opened in the candidate's absence and he is reintroduced by the Tyler. The candidate is 'proved' by being required to give the pass grip and password to the Inner Guard. With the Deacons standing on each side of him, he faces the Worshipful Master who says, 'Let the Candidate kneel while the blessing of Heaven is invoked on what we are about to do.'

The Worshipful Master continues: 'We supplicate the continuance of thine aid, O merciful Lord, on behalf of ourselves, and him who kneels before thee. May the work begun in thy name be continued to thy Glory and evermore established in us by obedience to Thy precepts.'

History has shown how graphically the name of God has been taken and used to perpetrate the most heinous of acts. Hitler's Nazi government duped the majority of people of a civilized country into believing that they were doing what was right under God. I am not, of course, seeking to compare the Nazi atrocities to the activities of freemasonry. My point is that it is all-too-easy to call on the name of God in support of some pursuit and assume that he nods his approval. This is probably the nub of the problem and may not be understood by a person who has not accepted Christ as Saviour and invited him to be Lord of his life. 'But a natural man does not accept the things of the Spirit of God; for they are foolishness to him, and he cannot understand them, because they are spiritually appraised' (1 Corinthians 2:14).

From the entry of sin into this world through Adam, man has had a knowledge that God did not want him to possess since it means inevitable death (Genesis 2:16-17). Man was created by God to live in co-operation, dependence and peace with his Maker. However, he rebelled and gained the knowledge of good and evil. Since that time man has sought to justify himself—to make himself right with God—by his knowledge, understanding and own interpretation of what is good and right.

But because something may appear to be, or may indeed be, good does not of itself imply that it bears the approval of the most high God. Let me illustrate it this way: suppose you are working for local government in some position where you have authority to sign large cheques—in payment for road repairs, for example. News reaches your ears of a terrible famine in some part of the world where millions of pounds are needed to give aid. You are deeply moved and immediately authorize a cheque to be sent from the council funds to the place of need. That, you feel, is a far better use of the money. You may also feel that you have done a fine thing in the name of the Council. But I wonder whether the Council would be so pleased!

> For My thoughts are not your thoughts,
> Neither are your ways My ways declares the Lord. . . .
> For all of us have become like one who is unclean,
> And all our righteous deeds are like a filthy garment.[4]

The name of God is not to be used lightly. We are not to use his name, to take it in vain, unless we are certain that it is his divine will. Freemasonry appears to most people as an eminently good, moral and upright institution, but can it be seriously believed to be furthering the ways and precepts of God when it uses the words 'in thy name'?

The prayer is accompanied by the sign of reverence, the right hand placed on the left breast with the thumb closed. This is very similar to the sign of fidelity which has the thumb squared upwards.

The candidate then perambulates the lodge, meeting the

Wardens in turn who examine him on his knowledge of the first degree. As the Worshipful Master observes the regularity of his initiation, he is then encouraged to demonstrate his knowledge of the pass grip and password leading from the first to the second degree. He is told by the Senior Deacon that 'the method of advancing from West to East in this Degree is by five steps as if ascending a winding staircase'. There follows a demonstration of a person changing direction by completing a semi-circle on flat ground as if climbing a winding staircase! The candidate must then repeat this action before the Worshipful Master, initially facing south with his feet at right angles, heel to heel, right foot pointing west and left foot pointing south, stepping off with the left foot first, completing a semi-circle in five steps.

The candidate is asked whether he is willing to take a further obligation, which he takes ceremonially on the Volume of Sacred Law, addressed to the 'Grand Geometrician of the Universe'. He promises to conceal the second degree signs and mysteries, and indeed never to reveal that he belongs to this degree, either to the outside world or to Entered Apprentices. He pledges to be a true and faithful candidate, to obey summonses and maintain masonic principles, under the traditional penalty:

> . . . of having my left breast laid open, my heart torn therefrom and given to the ravenous birds of the air or devouring beasts of the field, as prey, so help me Almighty God and keep me steadfast in all this my solemn obligation as a Fellow Craft Freemason.

The Worshipful Master responds:

> As a pledge of your Fidelity, and to render this a Solemn Obligation which might otherwise be considered but a serious promise you will seal it with your lips twice on the Volume of Sacred Law.

Masons vary greatly in their interpretation of the pact of secrecy that they have sworn. Some take it to the letter of the law and will discuss nothing whatsoever about what goes on behind the doors of the lodge with anyone who is not of equal rank. Others see certain parts of the ritual as the secret element that they are to keep to themselves (e.g. passgrips, passwords, oaths). A few talk about the lodge practices fairly openly, particularly if they feel that there is a chance that their hearer may join. The above statement by the Worshipful Master clearly indicates that the craft sees its ritual as being bound by secrecy in a far stronger way than a serious promise. It is to be a 'Solemn Obligation' which must be sealed with a kiss on the Volume of Sacred Law appropriate to the lodge or candidate.

The penalty for betrayal of the secrets, traditionally understood, or indeed explained, is fearful, getting more horrendous with each successive degree. This is, of course, in violation of civil law, moral decency, and spiritual commands, and apart from any other consideration breaks the undertaking given by the Worshipful Master in the first degree that the candidate will discover nothing incompatible with these 'duties'. Jesus knew what it was to receive the symbol of love in the Garden of Gethsemane from Judas. Arguably, Judas did not at the time see it as betrayal. The realization did not allow him to live with himself.

It is at this point that the candidate is informed that he has reached the midway point in craft freemasonry and he is entrusted with the secrets of this degree, being a sign, token and word. The sign is three-fold, firstly of fidelity, then of perseverance and finally the penal sign. The explanation of the derivation of the second is amazing:

> . . . is given by throwing up the left hand with the thumb level extended in the form of a square. This took its rise at the time Joshua fought the battles of the Lord, when it was in this position he prayed fervently to the Almighty to continue the light of day that he might complete the overthrow of his enemies.

We will see an increasing tendency in the craft degrees to impose legends on scriptural truths as if to give some secret or hidden knowledge which the Bible apparently fails to reveal!

The candidate is then given the second degree grip (or token) and the word, 'Jachin', which as in the first degree, he is told must never be given at length but by letters or syllables. After the candidate has practised these, the Worshipful Master explains that this word:

> . . . is derived from the right hand pillar at the porchway or entrance of King Solomon's Temple, so named after Jachin the Assistant High Priest who officiated at its dedication. The import of the word is, To establish; and when conjoined with that in the former Degree, strength, for God said, 'In strength I will establish this Mine house to stand firm for ever.'

There are several occasions in these craft degrees where God's name is taken in vain, particularly in the obligations and prayers, but here we have a clear example of words being put into God's mouth! This statement does not appear in God's revealed word. Solomon's temple was never intended to last for ever, nor was it God's plan to establish the temple of freemasonry as his for ever. It was probably not his plan to start it in the first place!

This is very serious. Freemasonry is clearly implying divine and eternal establishment, identifying its origin with Solomon's temple. It is significant that the temple God most cares for is that of his faithful people, whose bodies are the 'temple of the Holy Spirit' (1 Corinthians 3:16, 6:19, 2 Corinthians 6:16). For a Christian this masonic teaching in particular will lead him back into a corrupt and erroneous form of Old Testament legalism which centred on outward appearance and knowledge rather than inner conviction and conversion.

The candidate then proceeds around the lodge in much the

same way as in the first degree, demonstrating his knowledge of the sign, step, grip and password of the Fellow Craft. He repeats the false teaching concerning Joshua and the establishment of Solomon's temple. Having demonstrated his competence in this degree he is given 'the distinguishing badge of a Fellow Craft freemason (being an Entered Apprentice apron with two blue rosettes appended, one in each bottom corner). The Worshipful Master informs him that:

> . . . the badge with which you have now been invested points out that, as a Craftsman, you are now expected to make the liberal Arts and Sciences your future study, that you may the better be enabled to discharge your duties as a Mason and estimate the wonderful works of the Almighty. . . .

He goes on to explain the significance of the working tools of a Fellow Craft freemason:

> . . . as we are not all operative Masons, but rather free and accepted, or speculative, we apply these tools to our morals. In this sense, the Square teaches morality, the Level equality and the Plumb-Rule justness and uprightness of life and actions. Thus by square conduct, level steps, and upright intentions we hope to ascend to those immortal mansions whence all goodness emanates.

The Master of heaven said: 'Truly, truly, I say to you, unless one is born again, he cannot see the kingdom of God' (John 3:3).

The ritual concludes with an explanation by the Worshipful Master of the second degree tracing board.

The masonic commentator J. S. M. Ward whose series of commentaries on craft ritual, are still best sellers more than half a century after publication, wrote: 'This is the great lesson of the 2nd degree, that by ourselves and in ourselves, we can discover and realize God.'[5]

This is the lie that masonic ritual instils. It interweaves biblical fact with masonic fiction, often derived from the mythology of ancient Egypt, Rome and India, making them all on a par. It is easy to see how some people may come to believe any amount of plausibly written myth if it also contains a dash of biblical truth. As we look at the so-called Hiram Abiff we will see how this process takes on monumental proportions.

Master Mason

Before a candidate can be 'raised' to this third degree, the lodge must be opened as in the second degree, that is, at the place the candidate has reached so far. His proficiency in this degree must be tested to ascertain whether he is ready to progress. Lodges vary in the seriousness with which they take these rituals, particularly the immense amount of learning that is required to do them properly. Scottish Lodges are reputedly far less strict about rote learning than their counterparts south of the border.

Having been interrogated by the Lodge Master, the candidate is required to reaffirm the pledge of the two former degrees with particular reference to keeping the secrets leading to this degree. He is shown a new pass-grip '. . . given by a distinct pressure of the thumb between the second and third joints of the hand'. He is also given a further password 'Tubal Cain'. He will require these to gain admission to 'a Lodge in a superior degree'.

Having saluted the Worshipful Master as a Fellow Craft and Entered Apprentice, the candidate leaves the lodge, while the assembled Master Masons prepare to open the lodge in that degree. It would be usual for the Junior Deacon to display the tracing board at this point. The use of tracing boards varies greatly from lodge to lodge. Many do not use the one in the first degree depicting Jacob's ladder while at least one, I gather, keeps all three on permanent display. Most seem to use each one during the ritual it illustrates in order to demonstrate the lecture. Emulation ritual, probably the most common, gives instruction on when the tracing boards are used while other rituals make no reference.

While the candidate is being prepared (both arms, both breasts and both knees being made bare and both heels slip-shod), the Deacons lay a sheet along a line in the centre of the lodge a few feet in front of the Master's pedestal. On this sheet an open grave is depicted, and on its edges are skulls and cross-bones. Some lodges have a grave-pit built in (like a baptistry though smaller). It has also been known for lodges to use a coffin! Walton Hannah makes reference to 'real or plastic emblems of mortality' being used in some lodges.[6] There is no doubt that death is in the air as the candidate enters. He is introduced by the Tyler as hoping to progress '. . . to be raised to the sublime Degree of a Master Mason . . . .' He goes on to inform the Inner Guard that the candidate hopes to obtain the privileges of this degree: 'By the help of God, the united aid of the Square and Compasses, and the benefit of a password.'

This vital information is conveyed to the Worshipful Master who sanctions the candidate's admittance. All the lights are extinguished, except the one by the Master's pedestal. (I could not help being reminded of the words of St Paul at this point. He speaks in 2 Corinthians 3:18 of Christians on their pilgrimage 'being changed . . . from one degree of glory to another' [RSV]. The mason would seem to be going from one degree of darkness to another.) The extended compasses, previously prepared by the Immediate Past Master are held by the Inner Guard, firstly against the candidate's breasts, then above his head to show that he has so applied them. The candidate is brought to a kneeling stool by the Deacons and the lodge door is locked. He is told to advance as a Fellow Craft (by taking the step and cutting the

sign of this degree) and likewise as an Entered Apprentice:
'Let the Candidate kneel while the blessing of Heaven is
invoked on what we are about to do.'

The Worshipful Master continues:

> Almighty and Eternal God, Architect and Ruler of the Universe,
> at Whose creative fiat all things first were made, we, the frail
> creatures of Thy providence, humbly implore Thee to pour
> down on this convocation assembled in Thy Holy Name the
> continual dew of Thy blessing. Especially, we beseech Thee to
> impart Thy grace to this Thy servant, who offers himself a Can-
> didate to partake with us the mysterious secrets of a Master
> Mason. Endue him with such fortitude that in the hour of trial
> he fail not, but that passing safely under Thy protection through
> the valley of the shadow of death, he may finally rise from the
> tomb of transgression, to shine as the stars for ever and ever.

This prayer clearly sets out the aim of this degree. The
blessing of God is called down, his undeserved love is re-
quested to withstand some hitherto undisclosed time of trial
and to rise through this into eternity. This is a very clear
statement of what is expected to be the result of faithfully
partaking in the ritual that is to follow. The assumption
being that it is clearly linked with 'the mysterious secrets of a
Master Mason'. In Christian terms it is to do with new birth.

The candidate arises from the attitude of prayer and ceremonially walks round the lodge, saluting the Worshipful
Master and displaying again his knowledge of the grip or
token and word of the Entered Apprentice. Then he perambulates again, this time as a Fellow Craft. He stands with
the Deacons and is instructed by the Senior Deacon to show
the sign, passgrip and password leading from the second to
the third degree. When this and further steps and wheels
have taken place, the candidate is again presented to the
Worshipful Master, who responds: 'Brother Senior Warden,
you will direct the Deacons to instruct the Candidate to
advance to the East by the proper steps.'

The candidate is ceremonially taken to the north side of the lodge, opposite the sheet or grave and turns to face south. The Deacons stand either side of him. The Senior Deacon informs the candidate that the method of advancing from west to east in this degree is by seven steps, the first as if stepping over a grave. He demonstrates the procedure for the candidate to copy. This begins at the west end of the grave. The grave is 'squared' firstly on the north side, then the south and finally the east. Four steps bring the Senior Deacon, and then the candidate, in front of the Master's pedestal with the feet heel to heel in the form of a square, left foot pointing north east and right foot pointing south east.

The reason for the reference to the hour of trial in the opening prayer now becomes apparent. The Worshipful Master tells the candidate: 'It is but fair to inform you that a more serious trial of your fortitude and fidelity and a more serious Obligation await you. . . .'

In fact, as we shall see, the trial is merely symbolic. Any strain or test that it exerts on a candidate is probably to do with his willingness to be subjected to greater humiliation in front of others. The degradation of the first degree with its much pilloried 'bare breast and rolled trouser leg' began this process. The farcical stepping and signs continued it but clearly more is to follow.

He must first swear a further oath, this time with both hands on the Volume of Sacred Law, to 'hele [pronounced hail], conceal, and never reveal any or either of the secrets or mysteries of or belonging to the degree of a Master Mason to anyone in the world . . .' unless, of course, they can be positively identified as having attained this masonic rank. The commitment of the pledge is remarkable:

> . . . to adhere to the principles of the Square and Compasses, answer and obey all lawful signs, and summonses sent to me from a Master Masons Lodge, if within the length of my cable-

tow, and plead no excuse except sickness or the pressing emergencies of my own public or private avocations.

It is interesting to consider how many churches would seek such commitment from a new member. A good test of where a man's real loyalties lie comes when a church meeting happens to coincide with a lodge meeting. There are other factors involved in this common situation which many clergy lament, and we will consider these later (see chapter 11). For the moment those of us who are in leadership in the church would do well to consider the commitment we seek under Christ from those entrusted to our care.

Other undertakings are given, several of which repeat the former two degrees, in particular the commitment to help brother masons in any sort of need, together with their dependants. The penalty for betraying either craft or members' secrets is:

> . . . that of being severed in two, my bowels burned to ashes, and those ashes scattered over the face of the earth and wafted by the four cardinal winds of heaven, that no trace or remembrance of so vile a wretch may longer be found among men, particularly Master Masons, so help me the Most High. . . .

The obligation is sealed thrice with a kiss.

Having been instructed on the significance of the fully displayed square and compasses, the candidate is assisted as he steps backwards until he stands at the foot of the grave. There he receives an exhortation from the Worshipful Master:

> Having entered upon the Solemn obligation of a Master Mason, you are now entitled to demand that last and greatest trial by which alone you can be admitted to a participation of the secrets of this Degree; but it is first my duty to call your attention to a retrospect of those degrees in Freemasonry through which you have already passed, that you may the better be enabled to distinguish and appreciate the connection of our whole system,

88

and the relative dependency of its several parts.

Your admission among Masons in a state of helpless indigence was an emblematical representation of the entrance of all men on this, their mortal existence. It inculcated the useful lessons of natural equality and mutual dependence: it instructed you in the active principles of universal beneficence and charity, to seek the solace of your own distress by extending relief and consolation to your fellow-creatures in the hour of their affliction. Above all it taught you to bend with humility and resignation to the will of the Great Architect of the Universe; to dedicate your heart, thus purified from every baneful and malignant passion, fitted only for the reception of truth and wisdom, to his glory and the welfare of your fellow mortals.

Proceeding onwards still guiding your progress by the principles of moral truth, you were led in the Second Degree to contemplate the intellectual faculty and to trace it from its development through the paths of heavenly Science, even to the throne of God Himself. . . .

This exhortation is probably the best summary of the system of craft freemasonry. By its own profession, it is a complete system in itself which lifts a man out of apparent 'helplessness', teaching him a new morality and, above all, submission to God. I have quoted the first part of this exhortation at length since it is important that we get the context and detail and understand what craft freemasonry sees itself as being able to do. The clear assumption is that through masonry a man can stand before God in some way purified, and enabled to receive truth and wisdom, to his glory. If this were true it would render Christ's atoning sacrifice superfluous; his death for all mankind, a waste of time; his resurrection from death, a needless action; his ascension into heaven, an irrelevance. If this is to be believed then the very centre of Christianity is rendered obsolete.

The objects of this degree are to teach a man how to die: 'They invite you to reflect on this awful subject, and teach you to feel that, to the just and virtuous man, death has no terrors. . . .'

Masonry clearly takes on itself the properties of deepest religion and faith. The object of worship in this degree is the 'unshaken fidelity and noble death of our Master Hiram Abiff', who, it is claimed, was slain shortly before the completion of King Solomon's temple.

No character in Scripture is called Hiram Abiff. There is a character called Hiram who was involved in the construction of the temple (see 1 Kings 7) and this is the only one to whom any link with the masonic Hiram Abiff can be drawn. The Bible tells us that Hiram was brought at Solomon's request from Tyre. He was a widow's son and his late father had been a worker in bronze. Hiram had clearly inherited his father's trade, being filled with wisdom, understanding and skill in all bronze work. It was he who was responsible for much of the bronze work in the temple. In 2 Chronicles 2 this man is identified as Huram-abi. Apart from that, Scripture gives no more information about his work, his life, his further activities in Jerusalem or his death.

Freemasonry reveals a great deal about a man called Hiram Abiff, who was involved in all that his near-namesake did, but also very much more. Hiram, it is claimed, knew the secrets of the third degree and, it is claimed, was the victim of a conspiracy by fifteen fellow crafts, of whom finally three waited one day for him to leave the temple at the time Hiram went to worship. They positioned themselves at the eastern, northern and southern entrances and as he tried to leave they sought to elicit the secrets. At each refusal he was systematically attacked, first by a heavy plumb-rule, then a level and finally a maul. The candidate progressively acts out the demise of Hiram, following the Worshipful Master's account and the Senior Warden's directions. After the third blow the candidate is laid lifeless in the grave.

Attempts are made to raise 'Hiram' by means of the Entered Apprentice and Fellow Craft grip, neither of which is successful. The Worshipful Master explains that there is one further method, which he demonstrates. Thus it is, by the 'five points of fellowship', that the hapless victim is raised to life.

> Let me now beg you to observe that the Light of a Master Mason is darkness visible, serving only to express that gloom which rests on the prospect of futurity. It is that mysterious veil which the eye of human reason cannot penetrate, unless assisted by that Light which is from above.

Again, there is clear implication that divine illumination is available to gain victory over the grave:

> Continue to listen to the voice of Nature, which bears witness that even in this perishable frame resides a vital and immortal principle, which inspires a holy confidence that the Lord of Life will enable us to trample the King of Terrors beneath our feet, and lift our eyes to that bright Morning Star, whose rising brings peace and salvation to the faithful and obedient of the human race.

There can be no denying that at the climax of this, the third degree of craft freemasonry, there is the desire to give to the candidate the ability to receive peace, salvation and holy confidence.

But who is the Lord of life, or indeed the bright Morning Star? Clearly, for a Christian there can be no doubt about who is considered worthy of holding those titles. Christ has won the victory over Satan, by triumphing over death. He alone is the perfect sacrifice, whose death and resurrection have brought peace and salvation to mankind. Further, if Christ is to be believed, then he is unique, there can be no other.

However the ritual would indicate that such eternal security can be discovered naturally in some way, being inherently resident in everyone. It is claimed that as we listen to the 'voice of nature' the potential of that 'abiding principle' can be realized, so that we can 'trample the King of Terrors beneath our feet', and attain 'peace and salvation'. But St Peter boldly proclaimed to the Jewish Council: 'There is salvation in no one else; for there is no other name under heaven that has been given among men, by which we must be saved' (Acts 4:12).

This is the united witness of the whole of Scripture, and stands irreconcilably opposed to the false doctrine of free-masonry.

The ritual continues with the candidate learning the sign of horror, the sign of sympathy and the penal sign. He is told that the grip or token for this degree is the first of the five points of fellowship (previously used to raise him from the grave), and he is taught the others with their significance, together with the whispered password MACHABEN (or MACHBINNA).

The candidate withdraws to dress himself normally with the addition of his fellow craft apron, and he returns to find the lodge fully illuminated. An account of Hiram Abiff's death and raising is then given. (See Appendix 1, where this is quoted in full.)

This account, as you will see, has every appearance of being from the Bible, but is in fact almost entirely fiction. It shows how a religious society can take a tiny passage from the Bible, about a relatively insignificant character, and elevate him to almost god-like proportions. He is known as 'our Master' and in some ways is attributed with Christ's own life and actions. Yet John wrote:

> I testify to everyone who hears the words of the prophecy of this book: if anyone adds to them, God shall add to him the plagues that are written in this book; and if anyone takes away from the words of the book of this prophecy, God shall take away his part from the tree of life and from the holy city, which are written in this book.[7]

The Bible is God's revelation and is complete. To add to

it, or to take away from it, is a serious sin. The ritual of craft freemasonry does both. It takes away in that it denies the essential mediation of Christ for the world and it adds a new system, which is in fact an extension of Old Testament legalism, which purports to lead to salvation. St Paul came to realize that the most Law can do is impart a knowledge or an awareness of sin (Romans 3:20), but through the Law 'no flesh will be justified in His sight'.

Elsewhere, he told the Galatian church: '. . . if righteousness comes through the Law, then Christ died needlessly' (Galatians 2:21).

Christ's death and atonement did something that the Law could not possibly do—it brought salvation to mankind.

My other sadness is that we see how so much of what masons swear to keep secret, and which binds up so many fine men, is a knowledge which is almost entirely legend, fabrication, trivia or nonsense. Either that, or a deliberate contrivance in order to instil false religion.

8

The Holy Royal Arch and the higher degrees

There are more than one hundred additional degrees, or orders, that can be attained in freemasonry, so to do the remaining ones justice in one chapter is clearly impossible. However, since the majority of freemasons in this country have little or no knowledge or understanding of the non-craft degrees, an account of the Royal Arch and a brief resumé of the other main ones must suffice. More information can be obtained from Walton Hannah's second book *Christian by Degrees* and other books detailed in the bibliography.

Many of the so-called 'higher degrees' are conferred by title alone in this country. For example, of the thirty degrees of the Ancient and Accepted Rite, twenty-five are conferred by name, prior to initiation into the eighteenth and thirtieth respectively. Some within the craft seek to play down the title 'higher', claiming that they are higher only in the sense of requiring at least Master Mason's status as qualification for entrance. Some also require membership of one or more other orders, and/or a minimum period of membership. Each of these masonic degrees belongs to a masonic order which is independent, having its own government, organization and distinctive ways of according recognition of membership and service.

Only about 40% of masons go any further than the three craft degrees. For those who would progress further the most usual avenue is through the Holy Royal Arch (or 'going into chapter' as it is known by many within the craft). The Holy Royal Arch is the only other masonic order officially recognized and administered from Grand Lodge in London. Its officers are included in the Grand Lodge Yearbook, along with the craft degrees' hierarchy. This situation arose as one result of the Union of the two rival Grand Lodges, the Antients and the Moderns, in 1813. The Antients had practised the Royal Arch as a fourth degree, and as the two Grand Lodges came together it was agreed that this order would be considered a part of 'pure Antient Masonry', an extension of the three degrees.

There are about 2,700 chapter lodges in England and Wales, attracting about 6,500 new members annually. This compares with a total of about 7,500 craft lodges (of which only about 6,000 are active). Roughly 16,000 men graduate through the craft degrees each year. This means that the craft is numerically in decline at present after its growth following the two world wars.

The Holy Royal Arch

This degree, the Holy Royal Arch of Jerusalem, to give it its full title, can only be entered by a Master Mason of at least four weeks' membership. It describes itself as the climax of freemasonry and 'inspires its members with the most exalted ideas of God, it leads to the exercise of the purest and most devout piety. . .'.[1]

Staggering claims! It is because this degree sets itself up to such a position, and because the ritual itself bristles with potential spiritual problems and compromises for the Christian, that I have quoted it in full. This can be found in Appendix 2 and I would suggest that you read this first to get an overall 'feel' for the ritual, its aims and its context.

It can be seen that many of the features of craft freemasonry pertain to the Royal Arch. The setting is biblical. The three central characters are 'Zerubbabel', 'Haggai' and 'Joshua'. 'Ezra' and 'Nehemiah' also feature prominently in the proceedings. The activity centres around three men who allegedly arrive from Babylon, having been part of the remnant left behind following the return of the Jews from exile. Three passages from Scripture are quoted to give credibility to what would appear to be a factual event. Doctrinal attributes of God—his omnipotence, his omniscience and his omnipresence are acclaimed as the lodge opens round the Volume of Sacred Law.

The candidate is introduced and having reaffirmed a pledge of continued secrecy, he is entrusted with the passwords 'leading to this Supreme Degree'—AMMI RUHAMAH, which, he is told, mean, 'My people have found mercy.' In whatever way this is viewed it is very clear from the context that it refers to those with a special knowledge which they have found or discovered. 'Mercy' is used in its religious sense of compassion or pity being given by God. By the constant references to this God, the candidate is led to believe that he is 'the True and Living God Most High', the Creator of the world, whose Spirit can be invoked and expected in the proceedings.

Before the candidate is introduced, he is blindfolded (hoodwinked) and again this takes on new and deeper significance. The use of the blindfold in encouraging the candidate to understand that he is entering a new sphere of freemasonry, for which he needs 'light', is very important. Two passages linked together from Proverbs are read as the candidate kneels before the altar. They speak of seeking knowledge and wisdom, and thereby understanding the fear of the Lord and the knowledge of him. The candidate is led to believe from these verses that this is of vital importance and is intrinsic to freemasonry. He is instructed or encouraged to act upon what he has heard by reaching out in his state of spiritual darkness or blindness to take hold of a scroll whose contents 'for the want of light I am unable to discover'. This is part of a prescribed plan which points to the fact that while the candidate abides in freemasonry, this special revelation or light can be realized. Indeed the principal character Zerubbabel reminds the candidate that he is by nature 'a child of ignorance and error, and would ever have remained in a state of darkness, had it not pleased the Almighty to call him to light and immortality by the revelation of His Holy Will and Word'.

In the craft orders and in this ritual light and revelation always refer to that which is being discovered in freemasonry. Other light, the light of Christ, for instance, has been removed. Elements of his way can be found but always without reference to Christ. There is no suggestion, direct or indirect, that this special revelation can be found anywhere else.

While the candidate remains blindfolded he is twice symbolically lowered into a vault, there to discover a scroll containing some hidden truth. On the second occasion the first part of Haggai chapter two is read by 'Haggai'. In its context in the Bible it is a prophecy looking forward to the new temple—Jesus, the dwelling place of God. The old temple has been destroyed, the new temple, which is Christ's body —again to be destroyed but rebuilt on the third day—is to be the forerunner of those whose bodies will be temples of the Holy Spirit (John 2:19-21; Mark 14:58; 1 Corinthians 3:17, 6:19-20; 2 Corinthians 6:16). '"The latter glory of this house will be greater than the former," says the Lord of Hosts, "and in this place I shall give peace"' (Haggai 2:9).

Those who know and love the Lord Jesus will recognize the unique nature of this prophetic word of God as Christ takes his glorious place in the centre of the world's stage and in the believer's heart. He is, as Isaiah foretold, the Prince of Peace, bringing 'peace not as the world gives' (John 14:27). Haggai's prophecy was originally given to encourage those engaged in the rebuilding of the temple after the exile in Babylon, but clearly it looks beyond the physical building, to the complete and perfect fulfilment of God's plan for his people, both Jew and Gentile. The masonic ritual, however, lifts the verse into a fictional context, where knowledge and morality, and not Christ, are the key. The candidate is already symbolically building this temple, as he subsequently will discover.

It is not without coincidence that the principal activity of the candidate, while blindfolded, is 'to remove the keystone'. The corner—or keystone—of God's church is Christ (1 Peter 2:5-7). He is the most honoured and important part of the building. How it must break Christ's heart to see men who are called by his name involved in activity which removes him from his rightful place in order to establish another temple, this time made with human hands! The unwitting victim who symbolically casts aside the central stone, is acting out a blasphemous lie, an abomination of God's name and nature. This is spiritual wickedness and deception of the highest order, for the real secret that the candidate finds himself discovering is that of the allegedly 'most sacred and mysterious name' of God, signifying 'His Essence and Majesty Incomprehensible'.

With his physical blindfold removed the candidate joins with two sojourners who arrive at the lodge, allegedly from Babylon, seeking work. They claim impeccable lineage, the royal line of David and the princely tribe of Judah—the same as Christ—and are given humble positions as labourers, since the principal jobs are already allocated. However, with an implied reference to the fact that the original secrets were lost with Hiram Abiff's death, they are instructed to bring any discovery of significance back to the Grand Sanhedrin (i.e. Zerubbabel, Haggai and Joshua). It comes as no surprise that they make the discovery!

As the account of the Principal Sojourner is read, one cannot help noticing the similarity with the biblical description of the discovery of the long-lost book of the law in Josiah's reign (2 Kings 22:3-8). This was a discovery of vital importance, which changed the whole face of everyday life for God's people. It was like a completely new revelation. Clearly this is the significance that this ritual would like to assume.

The two sojourners with the candidate return to Zerubbabel to report their discovery. They have found a scroll which was 'a part of the long-lost Sacred Law, promulgated by our Grand Master Moses . . .' (!) But something which is apparently very much more significant has also been traced —an altar beneath whose veil appeared the 'Sacred and Mysterious Name of the True and Living God Most High'. Here again biblical fact is interlaced with masonic fiction. It was, and is true, that orthodox Jews are unable to pronounce the name of God as revealed to Moses—that right being reserved for the High Priest when he enters the Holy of Holies once a year. But what the three companions saw is more than was even revealed to Moses, or so it is alleged!

The principals, on confirming the truth of the discovery, agree to reward the finders by exalting them 'to that exalted rank held by your illustrious ancestors'. They are relieved of their working tools and clothed 'in robes of innocence'. The claim that accompanies this investiture is further proof of the spirituality intrinsic to masonic ritual:

> The robes with which you are invested are emblems of that purity of heart and rectitude of conduct which should always actuate those who are exalted into this Supreme Degree.

It comes as no surprise that a ritual which begins with the Christian Collect for Purity (from the Book of Common Prayer) while omitting Christ's name as mediator, continues with the assumption that an individual can stand in innocence or purity by virtue of marvellous works or good conduct. It does not make it true though—this is merely another form of spiritual deceit.

In the explanation that follows the investiture, the candidate is informed that this enactment has taken place: '. . . somewhat in dramatic form, the more forcibly to impress on your mind the providential means by which these ancient secrets were regained.'

This statement is highly important. Not only does it indicate that freemasonry seeks to be self-authenticating, but also it is claiming specific divine intervention!

The three long lectures which follow contain some significant information. Firstly, epochs of biblical history are clearly seen as of masonic import, even being dated by a separate masonic calendar (Anno Lucis—year of light). The epochs are described in terms of masonic lodges—the tabernacle as the first or holy lodge, Solomon's temple as the second or sacred lodge, and Ezra and Nehemiah's temple—the grand and royal lodge. The historical lecture makes reference to the working implements of the three companions. Some rituals spiritualize these, reminding them of the final judgement, about which there is 'humble but holy confidence'.

The mystical lecture makes reference to Moses' encounter with God at the burning bush (Exodus 3). It adds to the biblical narrative information about the particular way Moses supposedly hid his eyes, this being adopted as a regular sign on the grounds that it was 'accounted unto him for righteousness'. This is a total distortion of fact since Moses' *faith alone* was counted to him as righteousness, as it was with Abraham and the other Old Testament men of faith.

A similar addition to biblical truth comes in the instruction given by God to Ezekiel (9:4) concerning the mark to be placed on the foreheads as a mark of salvation. The candidate is told that it was 'the mysterious triple tau', whereas Scripture does not record its identity. The climax of the mystical lecture reveals the precise nature of the name of God, earlier discovered. The candidate is informed about JEHOVAH (the common misnomer for YHWH—but here assumed as his name). This name is found around the outside of the circle on top of the altar. Within the circle is a triangle bearing the legend JAH-BUL-ON. It is important to understand that up until at least four hundred years after Christ, vowels in the Hebrew language were not written down so a word was identified by its consonants. In the ritual the 'u' of Bul drops out and two 'a's are inserted. It is very clearly a reference to Baal, although several combinations involving these letters produce everything but his name! However, the candidate is told that the word comes from the Syriac, 'signifying Lord or Powerful'. Thus there can be no doubt about the true identity of this second word in the masonic name of God. Baal is linked with JAH (Jehovah) as one aspect of the god of freemasonry! The third part of the name—ON—is generally assumed to be the recognized abbreviation for Osiris. The ritual specifically confirms its Egyptian origin, and explains that it expresses the omnipotence of the Father of all as in the Lord's Prayer!

In June 1985 I was invited to take part in the BBC Radio 4 'Sunday' programme in discussion with Commander Michael Higham, the Grand Secretary of freemasonry who holds high office in the Royal Arch. When questioned about the nature of JAH-BUL-ON he responded: 'No, God is not referred to by that name you use, that word is an invention. It is a description of God in three ancient languages. It is inaccurate scholarship, but it's been existing in masonic ceremonial for some time. There is no attempt to unite gods of different religions and set that god up as a masonic god.'

It is an interesting strategy of the craft that, in the last few years, as more has become known about it, and it has increasingly had to be defended, this major stumbling block has been dismissed as either inaccurate scholarship or a mere description, rather than itself the name of God. The ritual makes clear that it is a most significant name, and whether inaccurate or not, it still has the force of binding a man from repeating it. Commander Higham's next response was so sad: 'I am not going to say that name because I've got a block about it, rather like the Jews with the ineffable word.'

It is not surprising though, that he could not utter the name; this inability is the result of the oath agreed between the Principals both at the opening and closing of the lodge. The tragedy is that this name is at the heart of the deception of this degree, which claims: '. . . all that is nearest and dearest to us in a future state of existence . . . inspires . . . the most exalted ideas of God, it leads to the exercise of the purest and most devout piety. . . .'

The whole degree is a web of biblical fact and masonic fabrication, a fitting climax to a religious system based on major heresy mixed with a liberal coating of morality, charity and respectability. It thrives on vague doctrines of God, making him totally remote, while at the same time exalting the brotherhood of man and human aspirations to immortality. The whole thing is summed up by the revelation explained in the legend of the Jewel, which may follow the Royal Arch ritual:

> . . . on the circle appears the legend Si talia jungere possis sit tibi scire satis (if thou canst comprehend these things, thou knowest enough). On the triangle is inscribed EYPHKAMEN (EUREKAMEN) Invenimus cultor dei civis mundi (we have found the worship of God, O Citizen of the world). . . .

Need I say more!

Mark Masonry

This is by far the most popular of those masonic orders which are not officially recognized by Grand Lodge. Although not regarded as 'pure' masonry under the 1813 Union, these degrees have continued since the eighteenth century. Many of the masons who belong to this order regard it as a completion of the fellow craft. In fact, in Scotland it follows on from 'passing' into the second degree. The 1,200 lodges are administered from Mark Masons' Hall, 86 St James Street, London SW1 and the organization is very similar to that of the United Grand Lodge. Indeed, the great majority of those who hold provincial and district rank hold similar positions in the craft.

The ritual contains two degrees, Mark Man and Mark Master Mason and they are conferred in the same ceremony. Legend has it that this order grew out of the ancient ceremony when every craftsman chose a personal mark with which to hallmark his own work. This mark was centrally registered. The ritual is a fictional continuation of the work surrounding Solomon's temple. The object of it is a search for 'the most important stone in the building' and focuses on Psalm 118 verse 22. Having found the stone, the promise of Revelation 2:17 is read out: 'To him that overcometh will I give to eat of the hidden manna and I will give him a white stone and in the stone a new name written which no man knoweth saving he that receiveth it.'

In this country the degree is open to anyone professing to be a Christian, which probably means the vast majority of the population! It is significant that although a considerable number of masons justify their membership because of these and other so-called 'Christian degrees', they are not regarded as Christian in other countries. Walton Hannah writes:

The Mark degree is no more Christian than the Craft. It can be allegorized in a Christian direction only by misunderstanding the exclusive character of Christianity, the uniqueness of our redemption in Christ, and the true meaning of faith.[2]

Nowhere is Christ named in the ritual, and the symbolism is very strange indeed, far from consistent with orthodox Christianity.

Royal Ark Mariners

Every Royal Ark Mariners' Lodge is attached to a Mark Lodge, and the 570 or so lodges are governed from the Grand Mark Lodge. Qualification is by membership of a Mark Lodge and meetings often continue at the close of such a lodge. 'Elevation into this degree commemorates the providence and mercy of God and relates to the legend of the Deluge. . . .'

The Worshipful Master is Noah, not surprisingly! He is assisted by Shem and Japheth as Wardens, and the setting is the ark. The ritual is rather like a nautical version of the craft degrees, for example 'Noah's' prayer says:

> . . . may we so conduct ourselves in the Ark here that when we are called hence by the Supreme Commander of the Universe, we may find a blessed sanctuary in the mansions of everlasting rest.

Again, the ritual is a concoction of biblical fact and masonic fiction. It is arguably more Christian than Mark Masonry but is again not seen as exclusively Christian elsewhere in the world.

Ancient and Accepted Rite

The origins of these rites would appear to go back to about 1740. They gained the title 'Scottish degrees' but they seem to have originated in continental Europe (particularly

France) and the Americas. Although they were introduced into this country some years earlier, the Supreme Council was not founded until 1845. The Order has now grown to more than 700 chapters. The Rose Croix, or to give it its full title, Knight of the Pelican and Eagle and Sovereign Prince Rose Croix of Heredom, is the best-known degree, mainly because it is the only degree worked on a regular basis by private chapters. The degrees of craft masonry form the first three degrees of the Ancient and Accepted rite, the fourth to the seventeenth being conferred in name only at the Rose Croix or eighteenth degree ceremony. The candidate acquires many illustrious titles as he enters this Order, including Perfect Master, Sublime Elect, Scotch Knight of Perfection and Prince of Jerusalem! He must have been a Master Mason for at least one year before being considered for membership, when he can apply for 'perfection'. Hannah quotes the ritual in full.[3]

The candidate is introduced by a man who purports to be thirty-three years old, nobly born of the tribe of Judah! The scene that is described is clearly that which took place as Christ was crucified. The candidate is told:

> The earth quakes, the rocks are rent, the Veil of the Temple is rent in twain, darkness overspreads the earth and the True Light has departed from us. Our altars are thrown down, the Cubic Stone pours forth Blood and Water, the Blazing Star is eclipsed, our Shepherd is smitten, the Word is lost, and despair and tribulation sit heavily upon us.

The candidate is required 'to assist us in our endeavours to retrieve our loss and recover the Word'. The Most Worshipful Sovereign prays:

> Almighty and Sovereign Architect of the Universe who dost penetrate the secret recesses of the hearts of men, purify ours with the sacred Fire of Thy Divine Love. Banish from this Holy Sanctuary the impious and profane; and grant that we, aided by

the Power of Thy Spirit, may be enabled to distinguish the precious metal from the dross, and may not be deceived in the choice of him we are about to perfect. . . .

The prophecy referring to Christ, the Suffering Servant in Isaiah 53, is read and while this is happening, the candidate passes round the chapter seven times and collects three letters—F, H and C. He is informed that these refer to the 'three fundamental principles of our Order—Faith, Hope and Charity'. The Most Wise Sovereign continues:

Assisted by these Virtues, we have no doubt that you will ultimately succeed in attaining the end and object of all our researches —that Word on which our eternal salvation must depend.

He goes on to define the three words in Christian terms.

A procession is formed in decreasing order of seniority to search for the lost word, but the candidate is barred from taking part because he is not in possession of the word. Instead he is taken, veiled, into the Chamber of Death whence he is lead out by Raphael—through skulls, bones and corpses, into the Red Room. This room is ablaze with light, and the candidate's search reaches its conclusion as he ascends 'the ladder which leads from Darkness to Glory and Perfection'. Since he is enabled to answer the questions put to him he finds the 'word'—INRI. The Most Wise Sovereign asks the candidate to approach:

Worthy Knight, I rejoice to confer upon you the reward you have so well earned, and I trust that, by the practice of those Virtues that have this day been commended to your notice, you will indeed be led to Him who is the Way, the Truth and the Life.

Walton Hannah comments:

The most deadly heresy of this degree lies in the fact that it is the candidate himself who symbolically achieves both light and perfection by his own efforts, not in Christ or Christ for him. It is the Candidate who . . . journeys . . . to his mystical resurrection in the Red Room. The prayer in the Black Room until recently contained the phrase 'grant that we, being solely occupied with the work of our redemption. . . .' And the Resurrection in the closing ceremonies is defined significantly as the 'hour of a Perfect Mason'. Our Lord's redemptive death is treated as a type and an allegory of the experiences which a Mason must undergo in his quest for light, not as a unique and objective act of redemption wrought for him by God. This is, of course, a purely Gnostic conception.

An address on this degree explains that 'the Rose is an emblem of secrecy and silence; in the Song of Solomon we find reference to the Saviour under the mystical title of The Rose of Sharon'. Here indeed, in this direct association of Christ with an emblem which (according to Masonry, not the Bible) signifies secrecy, is a further admission that this degree interprets Christianity in the light of a mystery religion of the type abhorred and anathematised by the early Church.[4]

The candidate is rewarded with reception of the order of the Knight of the Pelican and Eagle, and Prince of the Order of the Rose Croix of Heredom with the Seal of Perfection. An explanation of the badge and jewel follows, linking them with Christ. The candidate is shown the signs and words of this degree, together with the password EMMANUEL, to which the response is PAX VOBISCUM. Having taken part in a sort of communion involving bread, wine and salt, during which reference is made to the time when 'we ascend to join our great Emmanuel and are united with him for ever in a glorious and happy Eternity', the Prelate recites the Gloria in Latin and concludes the ceremony with the words 'Consummatum est', which is the Latin translation of Christ's final words on the cross.

On the face of it this degree is full of real and supposed Christian symbolism, but it is still highly questionable for a Christian to justify his membership.

1.   The Most Wise Sovereign, in describing the events of

Good Friday, affirms that 'since masonry has experienced such dire calamities, it is our duty, Princes, to endeavour by renewed labours to retrieve our loss . . . .' Christians call the day Christ was crucified '*Good* Friday'. Christ's death could only be a 'dire calamity' for a group or individual opposed to the redemption of mankind. It is completely alien to the Christian faith to link Good Friday with some sort of retrieval of the situation by works.

2. If this is to be equated with Christian doctrine, then it must be freely available to all. The gospel is not something to be kept deliberately secret.

3. Salvation, it is clearly implied, is dependent on the discovery of the word—it does not come through faith in Christ. But Christians believe that knowledge of information is not God's way to eternal life.

4. The masonic communion is far from scriptural, merely taking the elements and using them in a most indiscriminate way. There is no attempt at consecration.

5. As with other so-called Christian orders, the world governing body of this order in America has declared that this order can be received by those of every religion, and 'any degree that cannot be so received is not Masonry'.[5]

One further point is worth noting. We have seen earlier how masonic apologists claim that masonry has no sacraments and no doctrine. In his final speech the Most Wise Sovereign exclaims: 'Princes, we rejoice to have united in this Feast of Fraternal affection. May we henceforth treasure up the sacred doctrines of the Order in the secret repository of our hearts.'

The teaching format cannot be viewed as different, in any real substance, through the whole of the rituals, both in the craft or in the higher degrees. In this degree we see both reference to doctrine and practice of sacrament!

9

Can freemasonry be regarded as a religion?

What is a religion?

In answer to this question I suspect that most people would agree with Karl Marx's assertion: 'Religion . . . is the opium of the people.' George Bernard Shaw wrote, 'I am a millionaire. This is my religion.' Jesus Christ saw it in an equally clear-cut way, 'No one can serve two masters. . . . You cannot serve God and mammon' (Matthew 6:24). Jesus saw that service of God is the chief end of man and that worship of him should be man's religion. However he recognized that it was perfectly possible to worship the created rather than the Creator.

How often have you heard it said of someone, perhaps jokingly: 'It's his religion'? I found that to be true of some of the men with whom I worked in banking. For them, the bank was their life. It took first place in their time, effort and commitment; it was more important than wife, family or friends. Some people's religion is earning money. They may not be quite like Scrooge, gloating over it night by night, but their allegiance to it may be equally strong.

Religion is that which takes precedence in a person's life. It can be a person or a pastime, a calling or a career, and for some, a drug.

But freemasonry is not a religion, or so it says. In a statement prepared by the Board of General Purposes, and accepted by Grand Lodge, the craft asserted its own view of itself:

The Board has been giving the most earnest consideration to this subject, being convinced that it is of fundamental importance to the reputation and well-being of English Freemasonry that no misunderstanding should exist either inside or outside the Craft. It cannot be too strongly asserted that Masonry is neither a religion nor a substitute for religion. Masonry seeks to inculcate in its members a standard of conduct and behaviour which it believes to be acceptable to all creeds, but studiously refrains from intervening in the field of dogma or theology. Masonry, therefore, is not a competitor with religion, though in the sphere of human conduct it may be hoped that its teaching will be complementary to that of religion. On the other hand, its basic requirement that every member of the Order shall believe in a Supreme Being and the stress laid upon his duty towards Him should be sufficient evidence to all but the wilfully prejudiced that Masonry is an upholder of religion since it both requires a man to have some form of religious belief before he can be admitted as a Mason, and expects him when admitted to go on practising his religion. . . .[1]

Recent concern over the compatibility of the church and the craft has caused Grand Lodge to reaffirm this statement of the Board and circularize all lodges. Commander Michael Higham, Grand Secretary, when questioned on this subject stated that freemasonry could not possibly be considered a religion since it has 'no dogma, no theology'.[2] Other senior masons I have spoken to have informed me that since freemasonry contains no creed, no sacraments and no catechism it cannot be regarded as a religion, merely as religious.

Many masons are genuinely baffled when we ask this question since they reason that if masonry teaches morality and how to live a good life, then it should be entirely compatible with the church, which, they understand has the same ideals.

No one can argue that freemasonry has a fine record of help, support and care in society. The organization has been very generous in many spheres of society. On a superficial level, the church and the craft appear to share many ideals, but a far deeper question is involved. Does an organization which is seen to be meeting those ideals obviate the need for the essential faith which is at the very root of the church, and from which its life derives? Is it giving to many men a substitute which is seen to remove the need for faith in Christ?

I will consider this by seeking to answer three questions which will help us to evaluate whether freemasonry is a religion:

1. Does it give the appearance of being a religion?
2. Has it become a religion in the lives of many men?
3. Does it set itself up to attract religious allegiance by standing as a religion behind all religions?

1. Does it give the appearance of being a religion?

For some, sacraments and dogma or theology may be essential ingredients in any true religion. However, many world religions exist with no systematized dogma, nor indeed do they use sacraments. Within the Christian church the Salvation Army functions without the two main sacraments—baptism and eucharist. Many Christians know little of theology—merely seeking to grow in their faith, their understanding and their knowledge of God.

What are the features of a religion? Most have buildings where some God is worshipped, using prayers and religious hymns or songs. Most have some holy book and use it for instruction. Most have some religious leader whose responsibility it is to instruct and encourage, to teach and admonish. Many use religious symbols to heighten awareness of the object of their worship and have incense and candles. All give teaching on how to live life either in a better way, or in some way harmoniously with the God who is adored. Most seek to imitate or follow men who have led the way along the path of religious observance.

Freemasonry has lodges and a temple. It uses prayers and has its own hymns. It uses the Volume of Sacred Law appropriate to the environment it is located in. It encourages the worship of the God which the individual believes in and seeks to heighten awareness of this God by giving teaching about his true name and nature. It has a chaplain, a Worshipful Master, deacons, wardens, and an organist. It uses candles, incense and at one point foot-washing, as well as masonic working tools which are used as objects of instruction in morality and supposed godliness. It assures its adherents that if they follow its tenets they will be certain of immortality and a place in the Grand Lodge above. It teaches its own spiritual, mystical, historical and symbolical doctrines, using biblical fact as a springboard to masonic fiction and myth. It cites as examples of its system historical characters such as Solomon, Zerubbabel, Haggai, Joshua, Moses, Ezra and Nehemiah and the fictional Hiram Abiff, looking to them as examples to follow. Its lodges face east for spiritual purposes. It uses fixed forms of liturgy and an altar and focuses attention on heaven. The titles it uses to address members of its hierarchy are the ones used in the church to address the clergy (i.e. Most Worshipful, Right Worshipful, Very Worshipful, Worshipful). Belief in 'the Great Architect of the Universe' is essential. It admits to being 'religious'. It has every appearance of being a religion.

A few years ago, whilst away from home, I happened to see in a shop window a cheaply priced knife marked 'Swiss Army'. I was particularly glad about this, as I knew that my son wanted a Swiss Army knife, though it was far outside the reach of his pocket money. It had all the gadgets that I knew he wanted at a fraction of the price I believed he would have to pay. I bought it. On reflection, I should have been more wary (unlike masons I have not been taught to be cautious!) as the assistant told me that in no circumstances should more than one blade be out at a time. I did not appreciate the significance of that advice. Of course I passed on the information, but being young he forgot, and a little while later came to me in great sadness: his knife had fallen apart. Had he used it with more than one blade out at a time? Yes. It was now no good.

The knife had looked just right. The marking, the colour, the insignia, and the price—all seemed fine! But it was not the real thing. It was a copy and in the end it did not satisfy, leaving a nasty taste. I guess that every day cheap imitations are marketed and bought. We're all vulnerable.

2. Has freemasonry become a religion in the lives of many men?

The word 'religion' today is often used flippantly to describe some preoccupation. A widow tells me that her late husband's garden was his religion; a parent describes his son's obsession with the local football team as religion. I myself can look back to my early formative years and see the status I accorded sport or pop music, and recognize that both were worthy of the title 'religion' for me. Many things can capture our attention so that we worship the created rather than the Creator. This is idolatry—defiled and perverted religion— for we are allowing people or things to take the place that rightfully belongs to God, giving our time and attention to something we have wrongly venerated. It can be cars, cats or kids, drink, drugs or our job.

Now each of us has needs and desires which crave satisfaction or fulfilment. The most important of these is the need for God. We need to be restored to the relationship with him for which we were created. Objects of veneration can imperfectly take the place of God for a time, but deep within us is a need which can only be satisfied completely as we discover 'the real thing'.

Sadly, history is littered with those who have gone after gods who are not God. In our contemporary world we have seen the proliferation of cults which appeal to so many young people, and to which they readily give their all. We, who are a little older, may look on with a mixture of bewilderment and sadness at such misplaced zeal and commitment. We can see through the sham, we believe, so why cannot they? We can recognize the 'angel of darkness' as he masquerades as light.

Now it is important to make a distinction. It may well be that for many people Manchester United are a religion. They eat, drink, sleep, dream and live their favourite football team. To blame Manchester United for this would scarcely be justified. They do not hold meetings in order to gain the religious allegiance of people. They play football—and the fact that they do this very successfully attracts adoration. Similarly, manufacturers of motorcars sixty years ago did not conspire to make a product which would command idolatrous zeal. It is perfectly possible for an inanimate object or an organization to become an object of worship or veneration by accident rather than design. Everything within the created order can arouse worship, to some degree.

Freemasonry is the same. Many men give a great deal of their time and money to the craft. To do the craft justice, allegiance which interferes with normal domestic life and marital harmony is not only not encouraged, it is disapproved of. However, I know from interviewing many masons, present and past, that such an allegiance can exist. For some, it is the accolade of gaining position, for others the thrill of new experience through esoteric ritual and the collection of masonic honours and titles. Others are never more happy than at the 'festive board' and cannot get too much of the 'social fellowship'. Many 'masonic widows' adjust to the inevitable with a resigned shrug, accepting the material deprivation or marital separation.

Freemasonry has the power to attract religious allegiance, and all too frequently does.

3. Does it by nature set itself up to attract religious allegiance by standing as a religion behind all religions?

Just as I am confident that within the Board Room at Manchester United no sinister plot is being hatched to gain religious allegiance, so I am equally convinced that within the meeting rooms at Grand Lodge no gatherings take place with the expressed purpose of attracting men's worship. Whether such a conspiracy took place more than two hundred years ago, I cannot say. However, as we have seen, free-masonry is a religion for many men (whether by its own design or not). Also, it has every appearance of being a religion by virtue of its language, symbolism and ritual which are used in a totally religious context.

The question we are asking is whether the expressed aim or intention of freemasonry is parallel to that of the church, and if so, whether it seeks to compete with or complement the church. Sir John Cockburn (Past Grand Deacon of England, and Past Deputy Grand Master of Australia) wrote:

> Religion deals with the relationship between man and his Maker and instils a reverence for the Creator as first cause. Religions abound in observances of worship by prayer and praise. They inculcate rules of conduct by holding up a God or Hero as a pattern for imitation. . . .
>
> It would be difficult to say in which of these characteristics Freemasonry is lacking. Surely it abounds in all. Its ceremonies are elaborate and are unsurpassed for beauty and depth of meaning. They are interspersed with prayer and thanksgiving

. . . . If the title of religion be denied to Freemasonry it may well claim the higher ground of being a Federation of Religions.[3]

The Christian church is based on Christ, on him alone. He claimed to be the way to God, the only way to eternal life. He taught that no man can come to God without him (John 14:6). He came to show God to men (John 14:9), preparing a place in heaven for those who follow him and giving them abundant life on earth (John 10:10). He came to lead men to the true worship of God (John 4:24). It is as men seek first his kingdom that everything else is added (Matthew 6:33).

I have quoted at length and in detail from the craft and Royal Arch rituals to show how the declared objects of free-masonry in its complete system are virtually the same—but without Christ. They teach that immortality and the 'ethereal mansions of Heaven' can be attained through observance of the teaching contained in this ritual. This is a continuing theme which comes by progressive revelation. They teach 'the sacred and Mysterious Name of the True and Living God' which, it is claimed 'inspires its members with the most exalted ideas of God, it leads to the exercise of the purest and most devout piety'.

The views of Sir John Cockburn, quoted above, can easily be dismissed as one man's ideas, but can he seriously be misled in his interpretation of freemasonry's aims when free-masonry itself makes such claims? I am convinced that many men whom I have interviewed, who are strong churchmen, are most sincere in their belief that freemasonry is not a religion. But most of them have freely admitted that, sadly, for all too many men the craft does act as a religion, or at least takes over the priority of commitment that the church should have.

As we have seen, all sorts of jobs, interests and compul-sions become religions to many people. However, there is a difference between those who achieve the status of religion without it being planned, and those who actively seek to win the allegiance of men's hearts.

I do not suppose that any mason I have interviewed believes that the craft deliberately seeks to masquerade as a substitute for religion. The Church of Rome, however, has clearly viewed freemasonry as a deliberate threat to the Church. It sees an unfolding plan, masterminded by those in the seat of power within international freemasonry, to subvert and divert true religion. For the average mason today this would appear unthinkable, because in all likelihood it would be entirely outside his experience of a benevolent organization given over to friendship, charity and good works.

Let me ask you what may seem a ridiculous question. If you were to start a movement to undermine secretly the church, to usurp all allegiance and take away its authority in the life of its members, how would you do it? Perhaps we can learn from the knife I mentioned earlier, or that phoney bottle of Chanel No. 5 you can buy in Oxford Street? Begin by making it look like the real thing. People might get wary or suspicious if it were called church, that might be too obvious, but there is no reason why you could not have all the trappings: prayers, a sacred volume, hymns, chaplain, an altar, teaching, ceremony and mystery, candles and so on. Of course, in order not to make it too obvious, it would be wiser not to meet on Sundays, when the main worship of the church takes place.

'And what about the cost?' you may ask.

'Well, you can get away with slipping a few pence in the collection plate.'

'No, not that, the real cost. Christ demands our life. He desires that we surrender our life so that like St Paul we can say, 'I have been crucified with Christ; and it is no longer I who live, but Christ lives in me' (Galatians 2:20). That is the real crunch in becoming a Christian. Most people do not like that, nor even want to understand it. It means letting go of what I want.'

'Surely there is some other means of encouraging people to think that there is another way to get to heaven—by living a good life, for example?'

'If you don't make it too difficult, and assure them that this will make them all right with God, then that should be very appealing.'

'People will not need to listen to what the church says, and will just take those parts of the Bible that fit in with this new way.'

Temple and Solomon

A great deal of freemasonry is distinctly Jewish. We have already seen something of the Old Testament basis of the rituals but it goes much further than that.

The centrepiece of Grand Lodge, the headquarters of craft freemasonry in this country, is the temple. According to the official guide it was designed in the classic manner while at the same time deriving its shape from the endeavour to give the impression of a great masonic lodge. The two together make for a most unholy alliance! In fact, the interior of the masonic temple would appear to have little resemblance to the biblical temple, except for the naming of the two pillars Boaz and Jachin (2 Chronicles 3:17). However, such items as the Star of David, the Menorah and some general temple symbols demonstrate something of the Jewish influence. The spectacular bronze-doors retell the history of God's people from the Exodus to the building of the temple. On the out-side are scenes depicting the material aspect of the temple—the crafts preparing and conveying the materials to Jerusalem for the building of the temple, together with the inscription:

> Concerning the House which thou art in building, if thou wilt walk in My statutes and execute My judgments and keep all My

commandments to walk in them, then will I establish My word with thee.

This is from the word given to Solomon by God concerning his temple (1 Kings 6:12). On the inside of these 'temple' doors the spiritual aspect of God's relationship with men is depicted. A corrupted version of Isaiah 6 is found:

The Creator designing to bless man's estate on Earth, hath opened the Hand of His benevolence with good gifts, and the Seraphim, with twain they covered their feet, and with twain they covered their heads, and with twain they did fly.

It is somewhat ironical that freemasonry makes Solomon its hero. Although he was responsible for the building of the temple, it was he who led the people into forbidden associations with heathen nations and into idol-worship. The explanation of the first degree tracing board informed the candidate that Abraham, David and Solomon: '. . . did then, do now and . . . ever will, render the ground of Freemasonry holy.' It was Solomon who ultimately brought desecration on his own temple!

Women

There are close parallels between freemasonry and Judaism, particularly with regard to women. In temple worship women are tolerated but are not recognized as members. A woman cannot be counted as a person to make up the number ten for a quorum—which is the minimum required for a collective act of worship according to Jewish Law. A masonic lodge is said to be perfect when there are at least seven present. No woman can be seated with men in the body of an Orthodox synagogue, for her place is at the hearth and for her there must be no manual labour nor any man's work. Women are tolerated in freemasonry only in as much as they are admitted to the lodge on 'Ladies Nights' which

are always mere social occasions. Great care is taken to en-
sure that no women are admitted to the ceremonies and
meetings —indeed part of the initiation ceremony for the
Entered Apprentice—the bared left breast—is incorporated
to prevent female intrusion.

Others

There are several other Jewish religious parallels which I will
summarize below:

The halter	Sign of submission as a slave (1 Kings 20: 31-33).
	Token of submission at initiation of the Entered Apprentice.
Loosing the shoe	A legal procedure in Jewish law to confirm a contract (Ruth 4:7).
	The Entered Apprentice arrives in the lodge slipshod to make his confirmation of secrecy and loyalty.
Charity to your brother	Concern for those within your land, that is, for fellow Jews.
	Masonic charity and benevolence are a feature of the craft and much good is done, particularly within the craft. However, the Hebrew 'Zedekah' which means 'charity' can also be translated 'righteousness'. The giving of money can thus be confused with righteousness.
Chronology	Hebraic chronology is taken from the creation, estimated to be 3760 BC. This is added to the year AD to obtain the Jewish equivalent.
	Masonic chronology is taken from the generally held approximation of the creation (Archbishop Ussher's—4000 BC)

	and this is added to the civil year.
The level	A Hebraic standard, all on a level, linking us together in neighbourly love (righteousness in Isaiah 28:17).
	The level is one of the working tools of a Fellow Craft freemason (2nd degree) to teach equality.
The plumb-rule	In Amos 7:7-8 this symbol represents Israel, who had been built correctly, but is now out of line.
	The symbol in masonry stands for rectitude, truth and uprightness and has given itself to expressions like 'he's straight' and 'straight as a die'.
Working tools	According to Deuteronomy 27:5-6 and Joshua 8:31 working tools were not to be made of iron. The Talmud explains that this is because iron is the metal of warfare while the altar is the symbol of peace.
	Masonic working tools are never made of iron and are usually of wood.
Jacob's ladder	Referred to in Genesis 28:12. Jacob clearly recognized that he was at the gate of heaven (v. 17).
	It figures centrally on the first degree tracing board with the explanation: 'On the upper part of the circle rests the Volume of the Sacred Law, supporting Jacob's ladder, the top of which reaches to the Heavens; and were we as conversant in that Holy Book, and as adherent to the doctrines therein contained as those parallels were, it would bring us to Him who would not deceive us, neither will He suffer deception. In going round this

> circle, we must necessarily touch on both
> those parallel lines, likewise on the Sacred
> Volume, and while a Mason keeps himself
> thus circumscribed, he cannot err' (!)

I have no doubt that anyone quoting isolated parts of this chapter would have a field-day in showing that my so-called Hebraic parallels are present in any number of other cultures and ages. However, if the *whole case* is considered, then it can be seen that there is an overwhelmingly religious and particularly Jewish influence within the craft.

Conclusion

There is a great deal more evidence which I must omit for lack of space. However, from this, and from the earlier chapters, where we examined the craft and higher degree rituals, words and symbols, there is but one conclusion: freemasonry is shot through with all that is religious. It is a sophisticated religious system, combining biblical fact and fiction, having many of the trappings of religion. Together these seek to instil a knowledge of salvation and a path of piety by working divinely (and becoming a god in the ancient sense of the word). Freemasonry is nothing less than a religion, fulfilling all the criteria of a dictionary definition of that word.

10

Do Christians and masons worship the same God?

Each initiate into freemasonry is given a copy of the Constitutions. This book contains, amongst other things, the charges of a freemason and the general laws and regulations governing the craft. The first charge is to do with the one stated requirement for membership—belief in a supreme being. Entitled, *Concerning God and Religion,* it begins:

> A Mason is obliged, by his tenure, to obey the moral law; and if he rightly understand the art he will never be a stupid atheist nor an irreligious libertine. . . . A Mason is, therefore, particularly bound never to act against the dictates of his conscience. Let a man's religion or mode of worship be what it may, he is not excluded from the order, provided he believe in the glorious Architect of heaven and earth, and practise the sacred duties of morality. Masons unite with the virtuous of every persuasion in the firm and pleasing bond of fraternal love; they are taught to view the errors of mankind with compassion, and to strive, by the purity of their own conduct, to demonstrate the superior excellence of the faith they may profess. . . .[1]

We have already seen that freemasonry combines a strong sense of morality with a belief in a relatively unspecified god.

The priority is significant. The message of this charge and the underlying thrust of the ritual is the supreme importance of morality, together with some sort of belief in a god.

Now to answer the question—which I have been asked many times—'Do masons worship the same God as Christians?' We must first be clear in our minds what or whom we are talking about. Firstly, we must look at freemasonry (the organization rather than the individuals who belong to it). Freemasonry does not define its god in Christian terms. He is described as an architect or geometrician rather than creator. This is not mere playing with words. A creator is a person who creates something out of nothing, others use something that is already there. As Christians we believe that God created the earth, the heavens and the universe out of matter which did not previously exist. This links in with the church's traditional understanding of the birth of Christ. He is 'the only begotten Son of God . . . begotten, not made'. He alone shares this divine origin, being fully God. Now, the god of freemasonry bears little relationship to the Christian God. Were we to ask why it is, assuming that the craft has no intention of excluding the Christian understanding of God, that in freemasonry God is so emptied and debased that he falls far short of the biblical understanding, the answer would be that this is deliberate. It is so that gods from other religions may also be included. A well-educated English mason may believe that the masonic Supreme Being has some attributes of the Christian God, but the craft has quite deliberately defined god in a way that allows anyone who has a belief in some sort of god to be accepted as a mason. Thus, in theory at least, it is quite feasible to offer membership to a red indian or a practitioner of voodoo. This is not fanciful, since whilst I was in Malaysia I met a man who had been a mason (recognized by the United Grand Lodge of England) while having a power of death through voodoo magic. On becoming a Christian he had renounced both freemasonry and voodoo!

As I have shown in chapter 8, the masonic 'architect' is known by the name JAH-BUL-ON and that is, according to masonic definition, the name of god in four languages: Chaldean, Hebrew, Syriac and Egyptian. It must be assumed that the Hebrew name is JAH and that could be interpreted as the widely recognized abbreviation for the ineffable word. However, that God, the Jewish and Christian God, has made it abundantly clear in his written word that he is One, and there is no other (see Deuteronomy 6:4; Exodus 20:2-3). Thus, if the masonic god does refer to him it is sorely mistaken when it equates him with other gods, who are not God. If it does not refer to him, then it is blasphemy—taking and using his name in vain. The craft has never stated which. Recently, as this name has become more widely known by non-masons, those speaking for the craft have tried to allay criticism by describing it as mistaken scholarship! The fact that it stands at the pinnacle of craft freemasonry makes it well-nigh impossible to change. It is an idol, a false, man-made attempt at redefining God, and its position at the very heart of the craft, as the innermost secret, simply serves to show how freemasonry stands on a spurious foundation.

Now, we consider the beliefs of individual men who are masons. Of course, they are required to believe in God in order to be allowed to join. At no time is there any further inquiry into precisely what that belief is. They are merely required to concur with the masonic view as they go through the rituals. Thus, as we have seen, the doors are open to men of any religion, including pagan and occult. Whereas in this country there is an underlying Christian morality and outlook, in other lands the religious influence is very diverse. Lodges frequently use more than one Volume of Sacred Law and a man joining the craft may find himself standing next to someone uttering the same prayer, but to a very different god. Freemasonry unashamedly sees this as a virtue!

This is practical tolerance, and one of freemasonry's great strengths. It enables men of all faiths (who might 'otherwise have remained at a perpetual distance') to meet in ordinary friendship. Without interfering in the way they practise their religions it shows how much they have in common.[2]

I am not in any way condemning attempts to unite men (and women) across the national, cultural and religious divides. That is something we urgently need. However, Christ did not preach reconciliation at any price. There were times when he had to stand firm and would not compromise, the way of the cross being the supreme example. My contention is that it is simply not possible to stand alongside a non-Christian and utter a prayer which he finds acceptable because it obviates the need for Christ as mediator, without changing the whole basis of our faith. The cross has opened the kingdom of God to men whose faith and allegiance is given over to Christ. As Christians we believe that we are nothing before God and cannot spend eternity with him without the justification and absolution of Jesus. Oil and water can never mix! The god whom others profess may be so remote that he is of little or no consequence. He may well be a god of their own invention. Their god may be a Buddha or a job, sport or money. That does not mean we can deny them Christ's love, but it does mean we refuse to join in worship on their terms. By doing this we commit spiritual adultery.

This was clearly a problem in the Corinthian church. St Paul recognized the seriousness of the situation and the need for unequivocal action:

Do not be bound together with unbelievers; for what partnership have righteousness and lawlessness, or what fellowship has light with darkness? Or what harmony has Christ with Belial, or what has a believer in common with an unbeliever? Or what agreement has the temple of God with idols? For we are the temple of the Living God; just as God said,

'I will dwell in them and walk among them;
And I will be their God, and they shall be My people.
Therefore, come out from their midst and be separate, says
the Lord.'[3]

11

The lure of freemasonry

I found an old book in the British Library which bore the same title as this chapter. It was written by a clergyman, and in the foreword he explained the title thus:

> What is the lure of Freemasonry? There is something unique about it, a bond unlike any other, uniting men of all ranks, types and temperaments into a closely-knit fellowship . . . to attempt to analyse it, is like trying to draw a rim round a perfume. Who knows what it is, or how and why, unless it be the long Cabletow of God running from heart to heart.[1]

Clearly Joseph Johnson believed he had found something without equal—a mystical fraternity which satisfied his deepest longing. It is tragic that the Rev. Johnson had not found such fragrance in the church but only in a Christless organization. He is not alone in such worship of the craft. For many men it is a rich elixir and some speak eloquently of the merits and virtues of the lodge.

There is a well-known maxim, 'Once a mason, always a mason.' As one comes to realize the very powerful hold that it has on many men it is easy to believe that that statement is true. This is not merely to do with the secrecy but also with loyalty and commitment. It is, I believe, very significant that membership in the craft has always grown dramatically following a war. There is something very special about comradeship amongst men, particularly in times of distress or threat. The lodge has been for many an extension of the friendship experienced in service life or else in a profession which is very male-dominated. Today recruitment is still strong amongst the forces, old boy networks, banking, the law, police, local government and amongst shop owners. It is increasing from artisans in a common line of trade or business. Many lodges have been started as, or are developing into, distinct 'single-interest' groups.

One leading mason, a Canon of a London cathedral, told me that the real secret of the lodge is fellowship. I know what he meant, though I would hesitate at his choice of word. 'Fellowship' is the English translation of Christ's words describing a totally new experience of relationship centred upon his love, empowered and enabled by his Spirit. We have already seen how the use of religious terms can communicate the sense that freemasonry is a religion.

Having spoken with dozens of masons over the last few years, I am convinced that the overriding appeal is 'fellowship'—a term used by most masons, I suspect, to mean that their fraternity involves many 'jolly-good' fellows! This comradeship (I believe that word to be more appropriate) can arise very easily, particularly as men share the same secrets and do not discuss contentious issues such as religion and politics. It would be a very nice thing for everyone if all problems could be evaded and life could be so stage-managed that potential conflicts are avoided rather than faced and worked through. Nevertheless this 'easy', some may say unreal, atmosphere provides the basis for much of the appeal of the craft. It can appeal to men who like an evening 'away from the wife', about which she can legitimately, it is claimed, know nothing. This secrecy is obviously another aspect of its appeal. There is a tremendous sense of anticipation and drama as an initiate goes through the rituals. Secret knowledge or secret understanding is very appealing to our fallen nature. Most of us like to be 'in on something', whether it be local gossip or belonging to a group we value.

As a man becomes more involved, he will very likely find the rituals and the supposed secrets and knowledge they contain very attractive. It is amazing that most laugh off the debasing parts of the ritual with a dismissive phrase or gesture. I suppose that the logic is that because everyone else must have done it at some stage, it really cannot be worthy of too much consideration. To think a great deal about it would be too painful. It seems scarcely credible that many of the people we all know, and in all likelihood respect, have been willing to submit several times to such appalling humiliation. I must confess to wondering sometimes what would happen if the church were to make that a condition of confirmation! Again, it says something about the lure and appeal of the craft that I have never heard any mason question the need for the bared breast, rolled up trouser leg, and all the other equally degrading things.

I do not think it likely that many men join the craft because of the religious aspect. Most new members know little or nothing of what goes on in the lodge, particularly with regard to religious observance. However, there can be little doubt that many find the mystery and aura of the rituals very appealing. Some will go to other lodges as guests to see how the ritual is interpreted there. I have spoken to a number of men who have told me that the craft satisfies needs that the church fails to meet—for example, the need for ceremonial, traditional presentation and for a sense of mystery or 'otherness'. This heightened god-consciousness is undoubtedly a form of 'cheap grace'. It is the granting of God's blessing and assurance in a false, man-made, man-centred way. Its religious basis appeals to the instinctive feeling that we are good enough to save ourselves.

However, there are others for whom the rituals and religious side are of little or no consequence. Their aim may be promotion, preferment or 'a greater share of the cake'. Freemasonry, to its credit, frowns on such exploitation of its institution. The candidate is questioned officially on several occasions about his motives for joining. On the other hand, outside the lodge some will boast openly about their aspirations or achievements through masonry, whether it be the new contracts, the increased business or trade, or the backhanders! There is no doubt that the system can be used for personal gain. I well remember a sub-manager under whom I served while in banking, announcing to those in the office that from now on we would see his career take off because his initiation into freemasonry was taking place that very evening. Although a rather bombastic man, there was no doubt that he, at least, was serious! There are many masons who are genuinely horrified by this attitude, and would willingly disown or disbar such members. This side of the craft can easily be exaggerated by society. Any organization, particularly a church, will offer mutual help, not to the express detriment of others but to support and encourage brothers and sisters who share the same vital faith: the man who employs a church member in need, the woman who shares a box of groceries with another who is destitute, are healthy by-products of a loving, caring, committed group of people. However, when an organization puts up a veil of secrecy so that those involved in pornography, for example, can pay bribes in the form of lodge fees, without any danger of being traced, then clearly there is a problem.

This is, I believe, one of the main concerns of the Deputy Commissioner of the Metropolitan Police, Mr Albert Laugharne, who in a *Handbook of Guidance for Professional Behaviour* has strongly recommended that police officers refrain from belonging to the craft, since it militates against an officer being accepted as even-handed! In *The Brotherhood* Stephen Knight quotes several examples where this secret aspect of freemasonry has acted as a cover for questionable dealings. To people who are less than scrupulous, this can be a very real attraction to the craft. Again, to their credit, there are a number of masons who are most anxious to purge the craft and its reputation—but while this shroud of secrecy persists it is an impossible task. Evil men love darkness!

Many men love to join clubs, societies and interest groups, and freemasonry is very high in social standing. It has a prestige and style which are not enjoyed by Buffaloes or Oddfellows, for example. It is commonly understood that the craft has enjoyed a fair amount of patronage from royalty and nobility. Some find this a most attractive side of the craft. They enjoy those occasions when they can meet on equal terms with men socially above them. If they get into the right lodges they may even find themselves in a position higher than someone nobly born! It would seem that in recent years freemasonry has largely recruited from the so-called working classes. A more widespread affluence has enabled a wider populace to join the craft. Some within freemasonry regard this as a lowering of standards and are highly critical and suspicious. Freemasonry has increasingly broken down the cultural barriers, probably more successfully than the church has done. To its shame the church in the last 150 years has made little more than token gestures to welcome the poor and needy into Christ's kingdom, remaining middle-class and remote.

The church in recent times seems to have had a lifeboat mentality—women and children first. It is, I believe, very significant that Christ sought to establish his church with twelve men. The strategy that clearly followed was to introduce whole families to Christ's power and love. I would suspect that in the majority of churches today a man coming in from the street would find little opportunity to express his faith or discover his intrinsic worth before God. It is scarcely surprising that a large body of men find the lodge more relevant and appealing! Added to this, the craft would appear to be rich in good works. Grand Lodge, as well as individual lodges, will make no secret of the large sums that they have given away to good causes, as well as providing medical help, and education for many both inside and outside the craft. The church's image in this respect is generally not good. The man who is comparatively well-off and seeks to salve his conscience, may find an outlet within the craft for his philanthropic aspirations.

Finally, freemasonry appeals to those seeking security. I have no doubt that most of the masons I have met believe that they will secure a place in eternity. As we have seen earlier, the craft enforces the erroneous worldview that man has the power to attain the heavenly realm without recourse to a mediator. It is enough if he is good enough in his own eyes. The craft can also give security in a material sense. Arrangements are usually made to provide for dependants when the need arises. In the main the craft has a good reputation for caring for widows and orphans though this will, of course, vary from lodge to lodge.

Leaving the craft

Many of the factors which give freemasonry such a wide appeal will militate against a man leaving the craft. I have spoken to a number of masons who, when confronted by the challenge of Christ and the need to repent of their commitment to the craft, have found it desperately difficult to withdraw.

The most obvious reason for this is the loss of face before friends. In order to join the craft a man must have a formal proposer and seconder. At least one of these will need to be a good friend because he will be putting his reputation on the line about the suitability of the candidate. If someone proposes to withdraw it will appear to be a betrayal of trust, and he will experience a great deal of pressure. I have known of men who have felt it necessary to wait until the death of their proposer before they could resign. This pressurized 'hold' is not confined to those who introduced the candidate. News spreads. If a man submits his resignation from the lodge then others around him will very likely wish to question him about his motives. His reputation in the local community may suffer or indeed he may face a loss in revenue or business because goodwill is withdrawn. There is, of course, an underlying constraint stemming from the fact that these men are bound together in a common pact of secrecy sealed by a death pledge. This gives an extra dimension of mutual commitment. So, to break that, or to threaten to do so, even if there is no question of secrets being divulged, is taken very seriously. Those who have memories of secret pacts with childhood friends will immediately recognize the bond that such intimacy affords. More especially, those who understand and appreciate the concept of 'the body of Christ' as found in 1 Corinthians 12 for example, will know what it is to be linked as strongly as the limbs in a human body to others in Christ. Freemasonry, by counterfeiting Christian fellowship, causes many to experience a deep sense of brotherhood which can cause pain and hurt when broken.

Most men who have decided to leave the craft prefer not to make a clear break. It can be much easier to withdraw by missing lodge meetings and gatherings, perhaps with excuses, than to make a public break from the craft. If this continues for more than three years without payment of subscription fees, then the individual's membership lapses and he is deemed to have left.

On the face of it, freemasonry would appear to have more

to offer men than the church. This should not be. Jesus Christ came into this world to die for the sins of all men. He came to give them new life. The lure of the craft, though at present in decline, has served to challenge the effectiveness of the church. There is no reason why anyone should not be able to discover the abundant life of Jesus in his body, the church. Christ's church needs to experience again the power and love which God released on this earth in response to Christ's return to heaven.

12

Testimony of a former mason

Ronald, that is his real name, was brought up in India, returning with his parents to England at the age of thirteen. Ronald clearly remembers, as a boy, seeing his father in masonic regalia and feeling very proud of him. His return to England in 1930 was followed by attendance at his local parish church where he joined the Sunday School, then the men's Bible class and the choir. He married just after the war, living in a village just outside a country town in the West Midlands and became secretary of the Church Council, an office he held for ten years. His testimony is sadly typical of a large number caught up in a church which may well be able to distinguish good moral behaviour from bad, but seems unable to discern right from wrong spiritually.

It was during this time as PCC Secretary that I was approached by the Treasurer of the PCC to become a freemason. My father had been a mason and had passed through the Chair of his lodge and I knew that my eldest brother was a mason too, though I did not know his rank. So when I was approached by a member of the church, I had no qualms about joining—I felt that it must be okay. When I told the vicar that I was joining the masons, he merely said, 'Oh, you don't want to join that lot!' He never took me on one side to explain why! So I went ahead.

For my initiation, which was expedited, I feel, because of my father's and brother's connections—I was told I was a 'Lewis'—I invited my brother to come to the ceremony. My proposer was quite shocked when he learnt from my brother that he was a Grand Officer!

I must say here that I never questioned any of the things I heard or the things which I had to do, in that ceremony or in any of the others. I merely thought of these as play acting!

My initiation was in 1960 and I went through the three degrees of the craft lodge and then went into chapter. I attended what was known as Lodge of Instruction but which was really a Lodge of Rehearsal. I never attended any study circles or went too deeply into it. I did a limited amount of visiting of other lodges but never joined them—I could not afford to anyway—and attended the Ladies Night which each new Master held after his installation.

My lodge was a big lodge and it took eight years for me to get on the Steward's list and a further eight years of moving up each year to attain the office of Junior Warden in 1976.

During these sixteen years, I moved out of my parish to a country village, where I again became PCC Secretary, this time for seven years.

[He returned to his former village and rejoined the church.]

At my first Annual Meeting of the church there, the one churchwarden resigned and as I was already known, I was appointed churchwarden—there was no one else!

I carried this office for seven years, during which time we had several vicars or clergy as we were part of a team ministry. I served on the Deanery Synod and on numerous committees, none of which really dealt with the basic question of being 'born again' or the things of the Spirit. In October 1974 the then Vicar invited me, along with four other members of the congregation, including the Lay Reader, to a meeting with a group of people whom he thought it would be interesting to meet. I did not know any of these other people apart from one couple at whose home I had attended some Lenten meetings.

The meeting started at seven-thirty and we broke for coffee at about ten o'clock. During the meeting it was necessary for the vicar to find some Bibles for the people from his church. We had not thought to bring Bibles, but all the other group members were talking from 'the word'! When we broke for coffee one lady—Pat by name—came across to me and said, 'I believe you're seeking!' I replied to the effect that of course I wanted to know more about God!

She then said, 'The Lord has told me to lay hands on you!'

Not quite the thing to say in Anglican circles is it? But something inside me prompted me to say, 'Well, if the Lord has told you to lay hands on me, you had better do it!'

At this we moved away to the other end of the room and I sat on the settee. She laid her hands on my head and prayed in what I now know to be 'tongues'. Another lady then spoke in English—what must have been an interpretation. I cannot remember what was said but I felt a tremor through my body from my head to my feet! We then got up and joined the rest of the party and I eventually got home at midnight!

Up to this time, I had taken the Bible Reading Fellowship notes but had never read or studied them seriously—I had read the Bible mainly when I had to read the lessons in church. But when I woke up the next morning after this experience I had a burning desire to read the Bible, and this has not left me since! What is more, now I understood it! For the next six months I spent every spare moment reading the word and my wife could not understand what had happened to me. I did not force it on her in any way—she just thought I had gone berserk, I think!

In May 1975 Pat, who had laid hands on me, lost her husband in a cricketing accident and his funeral was held at my church. I had not seen her since the meeting but after the funeral I got to know her and she became my 'spiritual mentor' for my vicar really did not know how to help me though I was quite close to him and discussed church affairs with him. Pat took me to some renewal 'Come Alive' meetings where I first experienced choruses, heard 'tongues' both spoken and sung, and saw healings. My wife came to one or two of these, too. Pat also lent me such books as *Nine O'clock in the Morning* and *When the Spirit Comes* and I devoured these. My wife read them but did not understand them.

In December 1975 Pat invited me to a healing meeting where the visiting speaker was to be the Rev. Peter Scothern. I agreed to go and so did my wife, surprisingly! At that time my elder brother's wife who lived some twenty miles away was suffering from cancer. She had not been told this and I felt that God might heal her if she could come, so I invited them to come too. Again, surprisingly, they agreed. They were committed Anglicans who did good works.

When we got to the church we found a tremendous warmth of welcome and the praise and worship was something we had not experienced in a church before! At the end of his address Peter Scothern invited those who wanted to receive Jesus, or healing, or some other ministry, to come forward. I went forward to commit myself publicly, knelt down and closed my eyes. After the prayer I found my wife alongside me with my brother and sister-in-law! There was great rejoicing that night, I can assure you, for all our lives were changed from then on. My wife and brother certainly had the same burning desire for God's word as I had had and my sister-in-law was given the strength to ask what was really wrong with her. Then God enabled her to reorganize her life ready to join Jesus in heaven. She died in February, knowing him and his peace.

From this point on my witness within my church grew in intensity—I was continually urging the church group to more and deeper prayer; to seek the Lord Jesus; to move into evangelism and to hold parish teaching weekends. Whilst there was a certain amount of response it was very limited and there was a fair amount of resistance to change.

Meanwhile, on the freemasonry front, I was appointed Junior Warden of my Lodge in January 1976 and the first ceremony in February was to be an Initiation. For this I had to learn the 'Junior Warden's Charge' which, though I had heard it on numerous occasions during the previous fifteen years, I had never had to learn it in the lodge of instruction. As I was trying to memorize this charge, I came to the sentence, 'No other institution can boast a more solid foundation than that on which freemasonry rests.' The Holy Spirit said to me, *'You* cannot say that! You have Jesus as your foundation and he is more solid than that on which freemasonry rests!' Each time I tried to memorize the words, the same question came.

I did the Initiation in February and then there was another in March! Again the same thing happened. So I said, 'Lord—what do you want me to do?' and he said,

'Come out.' So after doing the ceremony in March I wrote to the Master—I find it very difficult to call him 'Worshipful Master' for I know I have only one 'Worshipful Master'—Jesus—and to the secretary of the lodge and the chapter and resigned.

The Secretary merely phoned me to say he was sorry about it but the Master wanted me to reconsider my decision and we had a meeting at a local inn. He told me that I had taken a solemn oath which was binding on me, to which I replied that I should not have taken it in the first place and in any case my commitment to Christ must override it! He then told me that my appointment as Junior Warden had not been unanimous as there was at least one officer (Past Master) who had reservations about me but that he, the Master, had overruled them. He was now going to be made to look a fool. He asked if I couldn't carry on to complete my year, but I replied, 'No.'

Following this, I considered what I should do about my regalia etc. I thought I should hand it in to the lodge for someone else to have, but the Holy Spirit told me in no uncertain terms that I could not do that! So I asked him what I should do and was told to burn it! I went up the garden and did just that—the regalia, books and case, and felt a load drop off my shoulders, so to speak. When I told Pat about this she said, 'Praise the Lord—we have been praying for you about this—even though we did not know you were a mason!'

After this I was at a prayer weekend with a group of business men from Birmingham Cathedral and was led to give my testimony about freemasonry. From this Canon David McInnes was subsequently led to give two talks on, 'Should a Christian be a freemason?' and he asked me to testify in the Cathedral, which I did. After it, one or two people came and told me I would be greatly blessed for doing so. On the other hand, others who were masons said they accepted what had happened to me but could not agree with me!

In 1977, the Lord started speaking to me about moving house again, and in his humorous way brought us back to the village and church we had left seven years before! However, I was now a new creature in Christ Jesus, and so was my wife. We attended the village church for two years and tried to witness where we could. The services were completely dead—no Holy Spirit influence—and the vicar was very cursory in his acknowledgement of us. After two years of this, the Lord led us to go to the Cathedral. When we left the village church neither the Vicar nor any member of the church called to find out why we were no longer going there! That was how far they were interested in the body of Christ!

In 1978 my wife and I went on a pilgrimage to the Holy Land which again altered our whole conception of what being a Christian really meant. Christ revealed to us what he had done for us on Calvary in such a meaningful way that we were never the same again.

We worshipped at the nine-thirty a.m. family communion at the Cathedral—people seemed more friendly there than at the local church. We endeavoured to witness there too.

In 1980 I enrolled for a course of study with St John's College, Nottingham but before I got fully involved in it, a chapter of the Full Gospel Business Men's Fellowship International was formed in the town and I was appointed its first President. This has been my mainstay for the past five years and my means of learning more of Jesus and the Christian life! We were certainly not learning very much from the Bible at the Cathedral—plenty about the social gospel but nothing deeply spiritual. The Dean did some studies on Hans Kung's book *On being a Christian* which I attended, but I am sorry to say that there was very little of

Christ in those studies, nor of the need to be 'born again'. One person there had difficulty in accepting the atoning work of the cross yet carried the cross in the Cathedral processions!

One day in the Cathedral some friends noticed on the bookstall a 'masonic Bible' and raised the question with me that surely this was not right. So I subsequently took this up with the Dean and during a personal interview gave him my testimony. I told him that freemasonry was of Satan. This he could not accept but promised to look into it. After several weeks of silence I asked him about the Bible and his reply was that he had looked at it—it was an ordinary King James Version with a lot of masonic history in the front. He did not do anything about it.

However, the next year I was in the CLC Bookshop in Birmingham when the Lord told me to buy a booklet called *Christ, the Christian and Freemasonry*. I was shocked and horrified at what I read there. As I mentioned, I had not gone deeply into freemasonry and so what I read was completely new to me. I felt the Spirit tell me to send a copy to the Dean and then not to stop at the Dean but to send it to the Bishop and the two Archdeacons. This I did with a short testimony to each of them.

The Bishop replied that he was not a mason but added, 'I know many clergy, some of whom I would regard as amongst our best men, who have found it possible to be freemasons . . . who have been able to make friends and influence people for good whom otherwise they would not have met or been on terms with'!

One Archdeacon never replied and the other informed me that he was not a mason. The Dean replied that as I had taken this action he would have to bring it to the Cathedral chapter. This he did and it was subsequently agreed that when the current stock was sold it would not be replaced!

I also took up the question of masonic services in the Cathedral but have not been able to get action on this—in fact the Bishop actually preached at the one last July.

In 1984 my wife and I went to the USA for an FGB Convention and stayed to visit several churches and fellowships in Arizona and California. The kind of Christian life we saw there was encouraging beyond belief—and when we came back to the Cathedral with its dead orthodoxy and lack of Holy Spirit fire, we could no longer continue there. Seeking the Lord's guidance as to where we should go, we were led to a church on a large housing estate on the outskirts of the town where there was a born again Spirit-filled vicar! We started worshipping there but very soon learnt that the Vicar had been resisted in everything spiritual he had tried to do. He and his wife were very battered! There was one other 'born again' lady there who also was on the verge of giving up. We did our best to support those three—I went on the PCC at the Vicar's request but soon discovered that there was real division between the Vicar's vision and that of the PCC. During the two years we were in the parish the Vicar made several initiatives but each was blocked through a total lack of support. One leading layman said to me, 'We shall not do any good till the Vicar goes'! The church was of the Anglo-Catholic tradition and they felt that they were losing their catholicity!

The Vicar finally looked for another living and has just moved, and we felt that it was time for us to move out too. But we wanted to be sure that this was God's will for us. Whilst doing my daily reading and prayer, I was led to Isaiah 52:11-12 and these verses just jumped out of the page! Hence we are leaving the Church of England.

The controversy about the Bishop of Durham, the lack of consensus amongst the bishops on the whole question of doctrine; the lukewarmness of the whole Anglican Church in this diocese in particular and the lack of true biblical teaching in the majority of the churches, has confirmed for me the apostasy of the Anglican Church. Yes, there are some Anglican churches which are alive but any that try to be in this diocese will soon be quenched.

I know personally one vicar—or as he is now euphemistically termed, Priest in Charge—whose licence was revoked mainly because he dared to be somewhat charismatic and teach about the things of the Spirit. I know another who suffered three years of torment from clergy of all denominations in another town for the same reason, and a third who as a curate was told that he would not get a living in the diocese for the same reason. I know of a Rural Dean whose set purpose is to quench any signs of renewal in his Deanery—he is of an Anglo-Catholic persuasion and believes in salvation through the sacraments! The Bishop thinks the Church of England is biblical because the Bible is read two or three times in our services! What is the point of reading it if you don't believe it to be true?

Since coming out of freemasonry I have been shown by the Lord that it is a totally counterfeit church. In the Full Gospel Businessmen's Fellowship I have given my testimony on several occasions and as a result a number of masons have come out, too. A man who was very high up in freemasonry came out, being 'born again' and filled with the Spirit.

I do not believe a nominal church-going Christian will ever see the faults in freemasonry. We have to be 'born again' and filled with the Holy Spirit who alone can lead us into all the truth.

As an Anglican vicar I could not stay in the Church of England if I believed it to be 'totally counterfeit' and apostate, but I do see so much of the life and vitality of the Spirit being quenched by tradition and maintenance of the status quo. The Church of England seems largely oblivious to the growth of the house church movement, and its relevance to today's generation.

Although we may not agree with all of Ronald's views, there is no doubting his experience of Jesus and his tremendous desire over many years to remain loyal to the Church of England. It was as he grew closer to Christ that the truth about freemasonry became clear. At a time when the Church of England Men's Society closes through lack of support, and attendance in church reaches an all-time low (matched with a decrease in resources) we must question the relevance and reality of what we, as a Church, present to those who are undoubtedly hungry for God. This is vital if we are to survive, let alone extend his kingdom.

Appendix 1

The death of Hiram Abiff

This is the final part of the third degree in craft freemasonry, delivered by the Worshipful Master and known as the 'traditional history'.

'We left off at that part of our traditional history which mentions the death of our Master Hiram Abiff. A loss so important as that of the principal architect could not fail of being generally and severely felt. The want of those plans and designs which had hitherto been regularly supplied to the different classes of workmen was the first indication that some heavy calamity had befallen our Master. The Menatschin, or Prefects, or, more familiarly speaking, the Overseers, deputed some of the most eminent of their number to acquaint King Solomon with the utter confusion into which the absence of Hiram had plunged them, and to express their apprehension that to some fatal catastrophe must be attributed his sudden and mysterious disappearance. King Solomon immediately ordered a general muster of the workmen throughout the different departments, when three of the same class of overseers were not to be found. On the same day the twelve Craftsmen who had originally joined in the conspiracy came before the King and made a voluntary confession of all they knew down to the time of withdrawing themselves from the number of the conspirators. This naturally increased the fears of King Solomon for the safety of his chief artist. He therefore selected fifteen trusty Fellow Crafts and ordered them to make diligent search after the person of our Master, to ascertain if he were yet alive, or had suffered death in the attempt to extort from him the secrets of his exalted degree.

'Accordingly, a stated day having been appointed for their return to Jerusalem, they formed themselves into three Fellow Crafts' Lodges and departed from the three entrances of the Temple. Many days were spent in fruitless search; indeed, one class returned without having made any discovery of importance. A second, however, were more fortunate, for on the evening of a certain day, after having suffered the greatest privations and personal fatigues, one of the brethren, who had rested himself in a reclining posture, to assist his rising caught hold of a shrub that grew near, which to his surprise came easily out of the ground. On a closer examination he found that the earth had been recently disturbed. He therefore hailed his companions and with their united endeavours re-opened the ground, and there found the body of our Master very decently interred. They covered it again with all respect and reverence, and to distinguish the spot stuck a sprig of acacia at the head of the grave. They then hastened to Jerusalem to impart the afflicting intelligence to King Solomon. He, when the first emotions of his grief had subsided, ordered them to return and raise our Master to such a sepulture as became his rank and exalted talents, at the same time informing them that by his untimely death the secrets of a Master Mason were lost. He therefore charged them to be particularly careful in observing whatever casual sign, token or word might occur whilst paying this last sad tribute of respect to departed merit.

'They performed their task with the utmost fidelity; and on reopening the ground one of the brethren looking round, observed some of his companions in this position [WM gives sign of horror] struck with horror at the dreadful and afflicting sight, while others viewing the ghastly wound still visible on his forehead, smote their own in sympathy with his sufferings. [WM gives sign of sympathy.] Two of the brethren then descended the grave and endeavoured to raise him by the Entered Apprentice's grip which proved a slip. They then tried the Fellow Craft's, which proved a slip likewise. Having both failed in their attempts, a zealous and expert brother took a more firm hold on the sinews of the hand, and with their assistance, raised him on the five points of fellowship, while others, more animated, exclaimed *Machaben* or *Machbinna,* both words having a nearly similar import, one signifying the death of the builder, the other the builder is smitten. King Solomon therefore ordered that those casual signs and that token and word should designate all Master Masons, throughout the universe until time or circumstances should restore the genuine.

'It only remains to account for the third class, who had pursued their researches in the direction of Joppa, and were meditating their return to Jerusalem, when accidentally passing the mouth of a cavern they heard sounds of deep lamentation and regret. On entering the cave to ascertain the cause they found three men answering the description of those missing, who, on being charged with the murder and finding all chance of escape cut off, made a full confession of their guilt. They were then bound and led to Jerusalem, when King Solomon sentenced them to that death the heinousness of their crime so amply merited. [WM continues the lecture by reference to the Tracing Board.]

'Our Master was ordered to be reinterred as near to the Sanctum Sanctorum as the Israelitish law would permit—there in a grave from the centre three feet East and three feet West, three feet between North and South, and five feet or more perpendicular. He was not buried in the Sanctum Sanctorum, because nothing common or unclean was allowed to enter there, not even the High Priest but once a year, nor then until after many washings and purifications against the great day of expiation for sins, for by the Israelitish law all flesh was deemed unclean. The same fifteen trusty Fellow Crafts were ordered to attend the funeral, clothed in white aprons and gloves as emblems of their innocence.

'You have already been informed that the working tools with which our Master was slain were the Plumb Rule, Level and heavy Maul. The ornaments of a Master Masons' Lodge are the Porch, Dormer and Square Pavement. The Porch was the entrance to the Sanctum Sanctorum, the Dormer the window that gave light to the same, and the Square Pavement for the High Priest to walk on. The High Priest's Office was to burn incense to the honour and glory of the Most High, and to pray fervently that the Almighty, of His unbounded wisdom and goodness, would be pleased to bestow peace and tranquillity on the Israelitish nation during the ensuing year. The coffin, skull and cross-bones, being emblems of mortality, allude to the untimely death of our Master Hiram Abiff. He was slain three thousand years after the creation of the world. [Reference to the Tracing Board ends here.]

'In the course of the ceremony you have been informed of three signs in this Degree. The whole of them are five corresponding in number with the five points of fellowship. They are the Sign of Horror, the Sign of Sympathy, the Penal Sign, the Sign of Grief and Distress, and the Sign of Joy and Exultation, likewise called the Grand or Royal Sign. For the sake of regularity I will go through them and you will copy me. [WM demonstrates the signs for the Candidate to copy.]

'This is the Sign of Horror; this, of Sympathy; this, the

Penal Sign. The Sign of Grief and Distress is given by passing the right hand across the face and dropping it over the left eyebrow in the form of a square. This took its rise at the time our Master was making his way from the North to the East entrance of the Temple, when his agony was so great that the perspiration stood in large drops on his forehead, and he made use of this sign as a temporary relief to his sufferings. This is the sign of Joy and Exultation. It took its rise at the time the Temple was completed, and King Solomon with the princes of his household went to view it, when they were so struck with its magnificence that with one simultaneous motion they exclaimed—'Oh Wonderful Masons!'

'On the Continent of Europe the Sign of Grief and Distress is given in a different manner, by clasping the hands and elevating them with their backs to the forehead exclaiming "Come to my assistance you children of the widow" on the supposition that all Master Masons are brothers to Hiram Abiff, who was a widow's son. In Scotland, Ireland and the states of America the Sign of Grief and Distress is given in a still different manner, by throwing up the hands with the palms extended towards the heavens and dropping them with three distinct movements to the sides exclaiming, O Lord my God, O Lord my God, O Lord my God, is there no help for the widow's son?

'I now present to you the working tools of a Master Mason. They are the Skirret, Pencil and Compasses. The Skirret is an implement which acts on a centre pin, whence a line is drawn to mark out ground for the foundation of the intended structure. With the Pencil the skilful artist delineates the building in a draft or plan for the instruction and guidance of the workmen. The Compasses enable him with accuracy and precision to ascertain the limits and proportions of its several parts. But as we are not all operative Masons but rather free and accepted, or speculative, we apply these tools to our morals. In this sense the Skirret points out that straight and undeviating line of conduct laid down for our pursuit in the Volume of Sacred Law; the Pencil teaches us that our words and actions are observed and recorded by the Almighty Architect, to Whom we must give an account of our conduct through life; the Compasses remind us of His unerring and impartial justice, Who, having defined for our instruction the limits of good and evil, will reward or punish as we have obeyed or disregarded His Divine commands. Thus the working tools of a Master Mason teach us to bear in mind, and act according to, the laws of our Divine Creator, that, when we shall be summoned from this sublunary abode, we may ascend to the Grand Lodge above, where the world's Great Architect lives and reigns for ever.'

Appendix 2
The Holy Royal Arch

The rituals show much greater variety in wording and instructions than can be found in the craft degrees. There is clearly much more local variation. The differences in practice mean very little difference in anything of substance. I have set out the ritual as I understand it to be most commonly used, so individual rituals will show slight variations in language but probably far greater in instructions for carrying it out. This is an amalgamation of three of the most common with minor amendments or additions by way of explanation.

The ceremony of opening a Royal Arch Chapter

The three Principals Zerubbabel, Haggai and Joshua stand in the west and give the knocks. They step towards the east, Zerubbabel in the middle, with Haggai on his right hand and Joshua on his left. They advance together, taking seven steps. At the third step they halt and bow, and Zechariah says: 'Omnipotent.' At the fifth step they again halt and bow and Haggai says: 'Omniscient.' At the seventh step they again halt and bow and Joshua says: 'Omnipresent.'

Z.   Omnipotent God, unto whom all hearts are open, all desires known, and from whom no secrets are hid, cleanse the thoughts of our hearts by the inspiration of Thy Holy Spirit, that we may perfectly love Thee and worthily magnify Thy Holy Name.

All   So mote it be.

Scribe Nehemiah hands small VSL to the Principals, who stand to order supporting VSL on their left hands, placing their right hands on it in form of a triangle, and repeating after each one in order Z., H., J.,

Z. H.   We three do meet and agree . . . in love and unity . . .
and J.   the sacred word to keep . . . and never to divulge the same . . . unless when three . . . such as we . . . do meet and agree . . . agree (Z) . . . agree (H) . . . agree (J) . . . agree (Z).

The three Principals kiss the Bible in turn, Zerubbabel doing so twice (i.e. first and last). They approach the east, and as Zerubbabel faces west, Haggai and Joshua join him to form a triple triangle, with right feet and with both hands. Their right hands are raised to form an arch. As they do this the sacred words are given in due form (i.e. syllable by syllable JE-HO-VAH, JAH-BUL-ON). They advance to their chairs, salute their sceptres and give the four knocks. Haggai and Joshua unveil the altar.

Z.   Companions in the name of the True and Living God Most High I declare this Royal Arch Chapter duly opened.

The ceremony of exaltation

The Candidate having been duly balloted for and elected.

Z.   Companion Principal Sojourner, retire and entrust the Candidate.

The Altar is re-veiled and the Principal Sojourner retires to the ante-room.

P.S.   Bro. A.B., advance to me in the three Degrees of Craft Masonry, communicating the words of a Master Mason on the Five Points of Fellowship. [Done]

P.S.   Do you pledge your honour as a man, and your fidelity as a Mason, that you have been raised to the Sublime Degree of a Master Mason for four weeks and upwards?

Can.   I do.

P.S.   Do you likewise pledge yourself, under the penalties of all your Obligations, that you will conceal what I am now about to impart to you with the same strict caution as the other secrets in Freemasonry?

Can.   I do.

P.S.   Then I will entrust you with the pass words leading to this Supreme Degree, they are AMMI RUHAMAH, the import of these words is, 'My people have found mercy.'

Principal Sojourner returns to the Candidate. Candidates were formerly prepared as for the third degree (i.e. both breasts, both arms and both knees bare, and both feet slippered). Now it is considered in most lodges that blindfolding only is sufficient. He enters clothed as a Master Mason. The Janitor knocks.

N.   Most Excellent, there is a report.

Z.   Companion Scribe Nehemiah, see who seeks admission.

N.   *(to Janitor)* Whom have you there?

Jan.   Bro. A.B., who has been regularly initiated into Freemasonry, passed to the Degree of a Fellow Craft, and in due time raised to the Sublime Degree of a Master Mason, in which capacity he has exercised himself for four weeks and upwards, and as a reward of merit has been entrusted with the pass words leading to this Supreme Degree to which he seeks to be admitted, and for which ceremony he is properly prepared.

N.   How does he hope to obtain the privileges of this Supreme Degree?

Jan.   By the assistance of the True and Living God Most High, the united aid of the Circle and Triangle, and the benefit of the pass words.

N.   Is he in possession of the pass words?

Jan.   Ask him.

N.   *(To Candidate)* Give me the pass words.

Can.   AMMI RUHAMAH.

N.   The import of the words?

Can.   'My people have found mercy.'

N.   Wait, while I report to the Most Excellent. *(Closes door)* Most Excellent, Bro. A.B., who has been regularly initiated into Freemasonry, passed to the Degree of a Fellow Craft, and in due time raised to the Sublime Degree of a Master Mason, in which capacity he has exercised himself for four weeks and upwards, and as a reward of merit has been entrusted with the pass words leading to the Supreme Degree to which he seeks to be admitted, and for which ceremony he is properly prepared.

Z.   How does he hope to obtain the privileges of this Supreme Degree?

N.   By the help of the True and Living God Most High, the united aid of the Circle and Triangle, and the benefit of the pass words.

Z.   Is he in possession of the pass words?

N.   He is Most Excellent.

Z.   Admit him.

The Candidate is admitted and placed in the west, between the Sojourners. The Principal Sojourner takes the Candidate's right hand in his left.

Z.   Bro. A.B., as you seek preferment in our Order, and have been entrusted with the pass words leading to this Supreme Degree, we must inquire if you freely and voluntarily offer yourself a Candidate for Royal Arch Masonry?

Can.   I do.

Z.   Do you present yourself with a desire of improving in Freemasonry, and directing that improvement to the glory of God and the good of man?

Can.   I do.

Z.   Are you willing to take a sacred and Solemn Obligation, restricted to this Supreme Degree, and if admitted, to keep inviolate our mystic rites?

Can.   I am.

Z.   Then you will kneel and receive the benefit of Masonic prayer.

The Principals give four knocks. The Candidate kneels. The Companions remain standing with the sign of reverence.

Z.   Almighty God, at whose command the world burst forth from chaos, and all created nature had its birth, we humbly implore Thee to bestow Thy spiritual blessing on this convocation, and grant that the Brother who now seeks to participate in the light of our mysteries may be endued with a portion of Thy Divine Spirit; may he not enter our Order lightly, nor recede from it hastily, but pursue it steadfastly; and may he ever remember that the object of our Institution is the welfare of our fellow-creatures, but, above all, the honour and glory of Thy most Holy Name.

All   So mote it be.

Z.   Bro. A.B., in all cases of difficulty and danger, in whom do you put your trust?

Can.   In the True and Living God Most High.

Z.   Glad are we to find your faith continued on so firm a basis. You may rise and follow your conductor.

Candidate rises. Four knocks.

Z.   Companions, take notice that Brother A.B. who has been regularly initiated into Freemasonry, passed to the Degree of a Fellow Craft and in due time raised to the Sublime Degree of a Master Mason, is about to pass in view before you, to show that he is a candidate properly prepared to be exalted into Royal Arch Masonry.

The Principal Sojourner takes the Candidate by both hands and, walking backwards himself conducts the Candidate round the chapter, and places him in the west immediately in front of the Sojourners' chairs.

Z.   As you seek to participate in the light of our mysteries, we must call upon you to advance towards the Sacred Shrine, on which they are deposited, by seven steps, halting and bowing at the third, fifth, and seventh, for at each step you will approach nearer to the Sacred and Mysterious Name of the True and Living God Most High.

The Principal Sojourner instructs the Candidate to take three steps, commencing with the left foot, halt, and bow; take two steps commencing with the right foot, halt and bow; take two more commencing with the right foot, halt and bow.

Z.   You have now arrived at the crown of a vaulted chamber, into which it is necessary that you should descend. You will therefore figuratively wrench forth two of the Arch-stones.

The Principal Sojourner takes a crowbar from the floor-cloth and places it in the Candidate's hands. He is instructed to make two levering motions, and then replaces crowbar.

Z.   Let the Candidate be duly lowered into the Vault, and attend to a portion of the writings of our Grand Master King Solomon.

The Principal Sojourner lowers Candidate on his knees before the Altar. Joshua stands and reads Proverbs 2:1-9 and 3:13-20.

J.   'My son, if thou wilt receive my words, and hide my commandments with thee;
So that thou incline thine ear unto wisdom, and apply thy heart to understanding;
Yea, if thou criest after knowledge, and liftest up thy voice for understanding;
If thou seekest her as silver, and searchest for her as for hid treasures:

158

Then shalt thou understand the fear of the Lord, and find the knowledge of God.

For the Lord giveth wisdom; out of His mouth cometh knowledge and understanding.

He layeth up sound wisdom for the righteous:

He is a buckler to them that walk uprightly.

He keepeth the paths of judgment, and preserveth the way of His saints.

Then shalt thou understand righteousness, and judgment, and equity: yea, every good path.'

'Happy is the man that findeth wisdom, and the man that getteth understanding.

For the merchandise of it is better than the merchandise of silver, and the gain thereof than fine gold.

She is more precious than rubies; and all the things thou canst desire are not to be compared unto her.

Length of days is in her right hand; and in her left hand riches and honour.

Her ways are ways of pleasantness, and all her paths are peace.

She is a tree of life to them that lay hold upon her: and happy is every one that retaineth her.

The Lord by wisdom hath founded the earth; by understanding hath He established the Heavens.

By His knowledge the depths are broken up, and the clouds drop down the dew.'

Z.   You will now endeavour to find something within the vault.

The Principal Sojourner causes Candidate to grope and places scroll in his right hand.

Can.   It is found.
Z.   What is found?
Can.   Something like a scroll of vellum or parchment.
Z.   What are its contents?
Can.   For the want of Light I am unable to discover.
Z.   Let the want of light remind you that man by nature is

the child of ignorance and error, and would ever have remained in a state of darkness, had it not pleased the Almighty to call him to light and immortality by the revelations of His Holy Will and Word. Rise, wrench forth the Keystone, and prepare to receive the light of the Holy Word.

The Principal Sojourner replaces the scroll (or lodges it in the Candidate's shirt next to his breast). He raises the Candidate from his kneeling position, and assists him, figuratively, to wrench forth the Keystone.

Z.   Let the Candidate be again lowered into the Vault, and attend to a portion of the writings of the Prophet Haggai.

The Principal Sojourner again instructs the Candidate to kneel. Haggai stands and reads Haggai chapter 2:1-9.

H.   'In the seventh month, in the one and twentieth day of the month, came the word of the Lord by the prophet Haggai, saying, Speak now to Zerubbabel, the son of Shealtiel, governor of Judah, and to Joshua, the son of Josedech, the High Priest, and to the residue of the people, saying, Who is left among you that saw this house in her first glory? And how do you see it now? Is it not in your eyes in comparison of it as nothing?
Yet now be strong, O Zerubbabel, saith the Lord; and be strong, O Joshua, son of Josedech, the high priest; and be strong, all ye people of the land, saith the Lord, and work; for I am with you, saith the Lord of Hosts.
According to the word that I covenanted with you when ye came out of Egypt, so My Spirit remaineth among you: fear ye not.
For thus saith the Lord of Hosts: Yet once, it is a little while, and I will shake the heavens, and the earth, and the sea, and the dry land.
And I will shake all nations, and the desire of all nations shall come: and I will fill this house with glory, saith the Lord of Hosts.

The silver is mine, and the gold is mine, saith the Lord of Hosts.

The glory of this latter house shall be greater than of the former, saith the Lord of Hosts: and in this place will I give peace, said the Lord of Hosts.'

Z.   You will now prepare yourself to take the sacred and Solemn Obligation, without which none can be exalted to this Supreme Degree (or admitted to a participation of our mystic Rite).

P.S.   *(to Candidate)* Support the Bible (or Volume of Sacred Law) on your left hand and place your right hand upon it.

Four knocks. Companions stand around the ensigns, and all give sign of reverence (or sign of fidelity).

Z.   State your name at length, and say after me:

OBLIGATION

Can.   I, A.B., in the presence of the True and Living God Most High, and of this Holy Royal Arch Chapter, duly constituted, consecrated, and congregated, of my own free will and accord, do hereby and hereon most solemnly promise and swear that I will always hele, conceal, and never divulge any of the secrets restricted to this Supreme Degree, denominated the Holy Royal Arch of Jerusalem, to anyone in the world, unless it be a true and lawful Companion of the Order whom I shall find to be such after strict examination. I further solemnly promise that I will not dare to pronounce that Sacred and Mysterious Name which may now for the first time be communicated to me, unless in the presence and with the assistance of two or more Royal Arch Companions, or in the body of a lawfully constituted Royal Arch Chapter, whilst acting as First Principal. All these points I solemnly swear to observe, without evasion, equivocation, or mental reservation of any kind, under the no less penalty, on the violation of any of them, than that of suffering loss of life by having my head struck off. So help me the True and Living God Most High, and keep me steadfast in this the

Sacred and Solemn Obligation of a Royal Arch Mason.

Z.   As a pledge of your fidelity, and to render what you have repeated a Solemn Obligation binding on you so long as you shall live, you will seal it with your lips four times on the Volume of the Sacred Law. Companion Principal Sojourner, you will raise the Candidate in due form by the grip of a Royal Arch Mason.

The Candidate kisses the Volume four times.

P.S.   Brother A. B.—now a companion of our Order—rise.

Z.   Having been kept for a considerable time in a state of darkness what, in your present position, is the predominant wish of your heart?

Can.   Light.

Z.   Companion Principal Sojourner let that blessing be restored to the Candidate.

The Principals stand in order with sceptres forming a triangle, the Companions stand round the ensigns, tilting them slightly inwards. The Principal Sojourner removes the candidate's hoodwink.

Z.   We congratulate you upon being admitted to the light of our Order, and it is with satisfaction we express our confidence that your future conduct will fully justify our partiality in having exalted you into this Supreme Degree, so truly denominated the essence of Freemasonry. You will now read the contents of the scroll you brought with you out of the Vault.

The Candidate takes the scroll and reads Genesis 1:1-3:

Can.   'In the beginning God created the heavens and the earth. And the earth was without form and void; and darkness was upon the face of the deep. And the Spirit of God moved upon the face of the waters.
    And God said, Let there be light, and there was light.'

Z.   Such, my newly exalted Companion, are the first words of that Sacred Volume, which contains the record of God's revealed will. Let us therefore bless, praise, and magnify His Holy Name for the knowledge vouchsafed to us, and walk worthily in the light which shines around.

You are now at liberty to retire and restore your personal comfort, and on your return to the Chapter the ceremony will be proceeded with.

The Candidate and the Sojourners retire, clothed as Master Masons and return to the Janitor who knocks.

N.   Most Excellent, there is a report.

Z.   Companion Scribe Nehemiah, see who seeks admission.

N.   *(Opens door)* Whom have you there?

Jan.   Three Master Masons from Babylon, having heard that you are about to rebuild the Temple to the honour and glory of the Most High, are anxious to sojourn amongst you, and assist in that great and glorious undertaking.

N.   Wait, while I report to the Most Excellent.

He closes the door, and with sign reports to Zerubbabel.

N.   Most Excellent, three Master Masons, from Babylon, having heard that you are about to rebuild the Temple to the honour and glory of the Most High, are anxious to sojourn amongst you and assist in the great and glorious undertaking.

Z.   Admit them.

They enter and stand in the west—Principal Sojourner in the centre.

Z.   Strangers, whence come ye?

P.S.   From Babylon, Most Excellent.

Z.   What is your request?

P.S.   Having heard that you are about to rebuild the Temple to the honour and glory of the Most High, we are anxious to sojourn amongst you and to assist in that great and glorious undertaking.

Z.   As no strangers can be permitted to assist in that holy work, we must first inquire who you are?

P.S.   Brethren of your own tribes and families, Most Excellent.

Z.   But are you not descended from those who fled when the City and Holy Temple were sorely oppressed, or are you of those left behind by the Babylonish General for the purpose of tilling the land?

P.S.   We would scorn to be descended from those who basely fled when the City and Holy Temple were sorely oppressed: neither are we of those left behind by the Babylonish General for the purpose of tilling the land; but we are nobly born, and, like yourselves, descended from a race of patriarchs and kings. Abraham, Isaac and Jacob were our forefathers. Most Excellent, we are of the royal line of David and princely tribe of Judah, who for their sins and those of the people were led into captivity, with Jehoiakim, their king, by Nebuchadnezzar, King of Babylon, there to remain for seventy years, as was foretold by the prophet Jeremiah. The period of our captivity expired in the first year of the reign of Cyrus, King of Persia, it pleased the Almighty to inspire that noble prince to issue the following proclamation: Thus saith Cyrus, King of Persia. All the kingdoms of the earth hath the Lord God of heaven given me; and He hath charged me to build Him an house in Jerusalem, which is in Judah. Who is there among you of all His people? The Lord his God be with him, and let him go up. We eagerly availed ourselves of this opportunity of returning to our native land, and have come up accordingly to sojourn amongst you, and to offer our assistance in rebuilding the Temple to the honour and glory of the Most High, who hath promised by the mouth of His holy prophets there to establish His Name for ever, and give peace to the whole earth.

Z.   We acknowledge your noble ancestry, and cheerfully admit you as members of our tribes and families. It only remains for us to inquire on what part of the holy work you wish to be employed?

P.S.   Any position to which Your Excellencies may be pleased to appoint us will be deemed an honour conferred.

Z.   Humility and docility are sure indications of merit, but, from the lateness of your application, the principal offices are already filled. We will, however, engage you to prepare the ground for the foundation of the second Temple, on the site where the first formerly stood; for which purpose you will be provided with proper working implements, but we must lay this strict injunction upon you: that should you during the progress of your labours make any discovery you deem of importance you will communicate it to none but the Grand Sanhedrin now sitting.

P.S.   We humbly thank Your Excellencies for the trust reposed in us, and pledge ourselves to a faithful discharge of the duties thereof.

The Principal Sojourner receives the crowbar, the Candidate the pickaxe and the Assistant Sojourner the shovel.

Z.   Go and may the God of your fathers be with you.

The Sojourners and Candidate retire. The Principal Sojourner has a rope round his waist, and two smaller ropes fastened to his wrists. They carry their implements of labour. Janitor gives knocks.

N.   Most Excellent, there is a report.

Z.   Companion Nehemiah, see who seeks admission.

N.   *(Opens the door)* Whom have you there?

Jan.   The three Sojourners who were sent to prepare the ground for the foundation of the second Temple, having made a discovery they deem of importance, are anxious to communicate the same to the Grand Sanhedrin now sitting.

N.   Wait, while I report to the Most Excellent. *(Closes door)* Most Excellent, the three Sojourners who were sent to prepare the ground for the foundation of the second Temple, having made a discovery they deem of importance, are anxious to communicate the same to Your Excellencies.

Z.   Admit them

Nehemiah opens the door. They enter.

Z.   Brethren we understand you have made a discovery you deem of importance. You will therefore communicate to us the discovery you have made, and the circumstances which led thereto.

P.S.   Most Excellent, early this morning on resuming our labours we discovered a pair of pillars of exquisite design and workmanship. Proceeding onwards, we found six other pairs of equal symmetry and beauty, which from their position, appeared to have supported the roof of a subterranean passage or gallery leading to where the most Holy Place formerly stood. Our progress was here impeded by the fragments which had fallen during the conflagration of the former Temple. These we cleared away, and arrived at what appeared to be solid rock, but accidentally striking it with my crow, I remarked a hollow sound. I therefore hailed my companions, when he with the pick loosened the earth which he with the shovel cleared away, when that which at first appeared solid rock proved to be a compact piece of masonry wrought in the form of a dome. Aware who had been the Architect of the former Temple, and that no part thereof had been constructed in vain, we determined to examine it further, for which purpose we wrenched forth two of the Archstones, when a Vault of considerable magnitude appeared to view. All being anxious to descend, we cast lots. The lot, Most Excellent, was mine.

My Companions then tied this strong cord or lifeline round my body by which to lower me into the vault; but being apprehensive of dying from damp, noxious vapours or other unforeseen causes, I took a smaller cord in each hand by which to give preconcerted signals, should I require more liberty, or wish to be drawn up. I was then duly lowered into the Vaulted Chamber. On arriving at the bottom I felt something like the base or pedestal of a column, with certain characters engraven thereon, but for the want of light I was unable to decipher their meaning. I then signalled with my left hand for more liberty, and on exploring the Vault, found this scroll of vellum or parchment, but from the same want was unable to read its contents. I therefore signalled with my right hand, and my Companions drew me up, bringing the scroll with me. On arriving at the light of day we found from the first words therein recorded that it was a part of the long-lost Sacred Law, promulgated by our Grand Master Moses at the foot of Mount Horeb in the wilderness of Sinai. The possession of this precious treasure stimulated us to further exertions; we therefore enlarged the aperture by removing the key-stone, and I descended as before. The sun by this time had gained its greatest altitude, and darted its rays with meridian splendour into the Vault, enabling me clearly to distinguish those objects I before had so imperfectly discovered. In the centre of the Vault stood a block of white marble, wrought in the form of the Altar of incense, a double cube. On the front were engraven the initials of the three Grand Masters who presided at the building of the former Temple, viz, Solomon King of Israel, Hiram King of Tyre, and Hiram Abiff—with certain mystic characters, and a veil covered the Altar. Approaching with reverential awe I raised the veil, and there beheld on a plate of gold that which I humbly conceived to be the Sacred and mysterious Name of the True and Living God Most High. I carefully re-veiled it with all respect and reverence, gave the agreed-on signal, and was again drawn up. With the assistance of my Companions I closed the aperture, and have hastened hither to communicate to your Excellencies the discovery we have made, and the circumstances which led thereto.

Z.   Your narrative bears every appearance of truth, but to convince us you must state what you saw on that plate of gold.

P.S.   That, Most Excellent, we must humbly beg to decline, for we have heard with our ears, and our fathers have declared unto us, that in their days and the old time before them it was not lawful for anyone to pronounce the Sacred and Mysterious Name of the True and Living God Most High, save the High Priest, nor him but once a year, when he entered the Holy of Holies and stood before the Ark of the Covenant to make propitiation for the sins of the people.

Z.   We admire your pious caution; and your conduct considerably increases our esteem. We will, however, depute two of our Companions, Ezra and Nehemiah, to accompany you to the spot, and their report shall determine your reward.

The Assistant Sojourner takes charge of the Candidate. The Principal Sojourner goes with Ezra and Nehemiah to the north west corner of the room. Ezra says to P.S.: 'State what you saw on that plate of gold.' P.S. begins and the words are shared in regular order. P.S. returns to his place. Ezra and Nehemiah advance by seven steps, no sign, halting and bowing at 3, 5 and 7. They remove the veil from the Altar and report with Reverential or Hailing Sign to Zerubbabel:

E.   Correct, Most Excellent, in every particular.
N.   Correct, Most Excellent, in every particular.

Zerubbabel consults with Haggai and Joshua.

Z.   My colleagues in office concur with me in the opinion that, as a reward for your zeal and fidelity in having discovered the long-lost secrets of the Royal Arch, you should be at once called to that exalted rank so long held by your illustrious ancestors. Companions Ezra and Nehemiah, divest those worthy Masons of the implements of labour, clothe them in robes of innocence and instruct them to advance hither, that they may be further rewarded.

The Scribes take the tools and replace them on the floor cloth. They invest the Candidate and Sojourners with white surplices. The Sojourners resume their Royal Arch clothing.

Nehemiah instructs the candidate to advance by the proper steps: after which the Candidate copies.

> Z. The robes with which you are invested are emblems of that purity of heart and rectitude of conduct which should always actuate those who are exalted into this Supreme Degree. We invest you [puts on the badge] with the distinguishing badge of a Royal Arch Mason. We reward you [places jewel on breast] with this jewel as a mark of our entire approbation; and hereby admit you companions among us: and decorate you [puts on the ribbon] with this ribbon, the insignia of our order.

Principal Sojourner hands the staff of Judah to Zerubbabel

> Z. We also entrust you [gives the staff to Can's right hand] with this staff of office which you will always be permitted to bear, unless 72 of your elders are present; and we hereby constitute you princes and rulers among us: and should you continue in the faithful discharge of your duties, you will by a regular gradation be entitled to a full participation in our secrets. It is in this part of the ceremony that the words are communicated. Excellent Companion Haggai, will you please assist? Stand to order thus. They are given on a series of triangles formed first by the right foot, second with the right knee, third right hand on right elbow, and fourth left hand grasping left wrist. The words are JEHOVAH, JAHBULON.

The words are communicated syllable by syllable (in due form). In lodges where the triangles are used the Principal Sojourner assists the Candidate. After this the P.S. takes the Candidate to the west, gives Reverential or Hailing Sign and both face east.

> P.S. Thus invested, rewarded, decorated, and entrusted by Your Excellencies, it shall ever be our study to merit a continuance of your approbation by faithfully and assiduously discharging the duties of the high vocation to which you have this day been pleased to call us.

Z.   We congratulate you on being exalted into Royal Arch
       Masonry, at once the foundation and keystone of the
       whole Masonic structure. You may perhaps imagine you
       have this day taken a Fourth Degree in Freemasonry;
       such, however, is not the case. It is the Master Mason's
       Degree completed, for when you were raised to the
       Third Degree, you were informed that by the untimely
       death of our Master Hiram Abiff the secrets of a Master
       Mason were lost, and that certain substituted secrets
       were adopted to distinguish the Master Mason, until time
       or circumstances should restore the genuine. These
       secrets were lost for a period of nearly five hundred
       years, and were regained in the manner which has just
       been described to you, somewhat in a dramatic form, the
       more forcibly to impress on your mind the providential
       means by which those ancient secrets were regained. We
       have now arrived at that part of the ceremony when
       Excellent Companion Joshua will give the Historical
       lecture, Excellent Companion Haggai the Symbolical,
       after which I will explain the Mystical portion of this
       Supreme Degree. Be seated. Companions, I claim your
       attention for Excellent Companion Joshua for the His-
       torical Lecture. *(The principals knock)*

Address of the Third Chair—The Historical Lecture

J.   Companions, there are three epochs in the history of
       Freemasonry which particularly merit your attention.
       They are, the history of the first or Holy Lodge, the
       second or Sacred Lodge, and the third, or Grand and
       Royal Lodge.
          The first or Holy Lodge was opened Anno Lucis 2515,
       two years after the exodus of the children of Israel from
       their Egyptian bondage by Moses, Aholiab, and Beza-
       leel, on consecrated ground at the foot of Mount Horeb
       in the wilderness of Sinai, where the children of Israel
       pitched their tents and gathered themselves together to
       offer up praises and thanksgivings to the Most High for
       their signal deliverance from the hands of the Egyptians.

There, but before that time, the Almighty was pleased to reveal Himself to His faithful servant Moses, and to commission him His high ambassador, of wrath to Pharaoh and his people, but of freedom and salvation to the house of Jacob. There were delivered those mysterious forms and prototypes, the tabernacles, the ark of the covenant, and the tables of the Sacred Law engraven by the finger of the Most High, with sublime and comprehensive precepts of moral and religous duty. There also were dictated, by His unerring wisdom, those peculiar forms of civil and religious polity, which by separating His once favoured people from all other nations, consecrated Israel a chosen vessel to His service. For these reasons this was designated the first or Holy Lodge. Solomon King of Israel, Hiram King of Tyre, and Hiram Abiff presided over the second or Sacred Lodge, which was opened Anno Lucis 2992, in the bosom of the holy Mount Moriah, on the very centre of the ground where the solemn sanctuary of the Sanhedrim was afterwards erected. On that consecrated spot Abraham proved his intuitive faith by not refusing to offer up his beloved son Isaac, a destined victim on the altar of his God, when it pleased the Almighty to provide a more agreeable sacrifice. There, on the threshing floor of Araunah the Jebusite, David offered up the mediatorial sacrifice by which the plague was stayed. And there, in a vision, were revealed to him the plans of that magnificent Temple afterwards erected by his illustrious son, of whom God said, 'He shall build a house for My Name, and I will stablish the throne of his kingdom for ever.' For these reasons this was denominated the second, or Sacred Lodge.

The third, or Grand Royal Lodge, was holden at Jerusalem and opened Anno Lucis 3469, shortly after the return of the children of Israel from their Babylonish captivity, by Zerubbabel, prince of the people, Haggai the prophet, and Joshua the son of Josedech, the High Priest. Then it was that the kingly power was restored in the person of Zerubbabel to the royal line of David and princely tribe of Judah. Nor was all vestige thereof again effaced until after the destruction of Jerusalem by the Romans under Titus in the seventieth year of the present era. Therefore, to commemorate the restoration, this was called the third, or Grand and Royal Lodge, and we have in the present Chapter a resemblance of those grand originals. In every regular, well-formed and properly constituted Royal Arch Chapter we acknowledge the representation of the Grand and Holy Royal Arch Chapter at Jerusalem. The three Principals represent Zerubbabel, Haggai, and Joshua, whose names they bear. The two Scribes represent Ezra and Nehemiah, Lectors and Expounders of the Sacred Law and attendants on the Grand Sanhedrim, their names are likewise conspicuous. Yourselves represent the Sojourners, who for their zeal and fidelity in having discovered the secrets of the Royal Arch, were rewarded with seats among the princes and rulers of the people, represented by the rest of the Companions. *(Principals give four knocks)* Companions I claim your attention to Excellent Companion Haggai for the Symbolic Lecture. *(Knocks again)*

The Address of the Second Chair—Symbolical lecture

H.   Companions, the forms, symbols, and ornaments of Royal Arch Masonry, together with the rites and ceremonies at present in practice amongst us, were adopted by our predecessors at the building of the second Temple, as well to preserve in our minds the Providential means by which those ancient secrets were regained, as to impress on our hearts those exalted lessons of morality which we, as members of this Supreme Degree, are bound to practice.

    The form of a Royal Arch Chapter, when properly arranged, approaches, as nearly as circumstances will permit, that of a Catenarian Arch. Thus we preserve a memorial of the vaulted shrine in which the Sacred Word was deposited, whilst from the impenetrable nature of this the strongest of all the architectural forms we learn the necessity of guarding our mysteries from profanation by the most inviolable secrecy. It also strongly typifies that invariable adherence to social order and spirit of fraternal union, which have given energy and permanency to the whole constitution of Freemasonry, thus enabling it to survive the wreck of mighty empires, and resist the destroying hand of time. And as the subordinate members of the Catenarian Arch naturally gravitate towards the centre, or keystone, which compresses and binds the whole structure together, so are we taught to look up with reverence and submit with cheerfulness, to every lawfully constituted authority, whether it be of civil or Masonic regulation.

The keystone of the Arch is represented by the three Principals of the Chapter. For as the secrets of the Royal Arch were only regained by wrenching forth the keystone thereof, so a perfect knowledge of this Supreme Degree can no otherwise be obtained than by passing through those several chairs.

Haggai points to the chairs and goes to the side of the altar.

H.   In Royal Arch Masonry we acknowledge six lights, three lesser, and three greater. The three lesser represent the light of the law and the prophets, and by their number allude to the Patriarchal, Mosaical; and Prophetical dispensations. The three greater represent the Sacred Word itself, and are emblematical of the creative, preservative, and annihilative powers of the Deity. These lights are arranged in the form of an equilateral triangle, each of the lesser bisecting the line formed by two of the greater, thus geometrically dividing the greater triangle into three lesser triangles at the extremities, and forming a fourth in the centre, all equal and equilateral. This symbolical arrangement corresponds to the mysterious triple tau which has two right angles at each of the exterior lines, and two in the centre, in all eight right angles corresponding in number with those contained in the four triangles, for the three angles of every triangle are together equal to two right angles. It also serves to illustrate the jewel worn by the Companions, which forms by its intersections a given number of angles; these may be taken in five several combinations, and when reduced to their amount in right angles, will be found equal to the five regular Platonic bodies, representing the four elements and the sphere of the Universe.

The ribbon worn by the Companions is a sacred emblem, denoting light, being composed of two of the principal colours with which the veils of the Temple and Tabernacle were interwoven. Its sacredness is further signified by its irradiated form; it has even been considered an emblem of regal dignity and power.

The ensigns on the staves borne by the Companions are the distinctive bearings of the twelve tribes of Israel, and are figurative of a peculiar blessing bequeathed to each by the patriarch Jacob, who, shortly before his death, assembled his sons together for that purpose, as we find recorded in the forty-ninth chapter of Genesis; the tribes are further pointed out in the second chapter of the Book of Numbers. The four principal banners represent the leading standards of the four divisions of the army of Israel. They bear devices of a man, a lion, an ox, and an eagle: a man, to personify intelligence and understanding; a lion, to represent strength and power; an ox, to denote the ministration of patience and assiduity; and an eagle to indicate the promptness and celerity with which the will and pleasure of the great I AM are ever executed. The bearings on the sceptres denote the regal, prophetical, and sacerdotal offices, all of which ever were, and still ought to be, conferred in a peculiar manner, accompanied by the communication of particular secrets.

The Bible, Square, and Compasses are the appropriate emblems of the three Grand Masters, who presided at the building of the former Temple: the Bible denotes the wisdom of King Solomon; the Square the strength of

King Hiram; and the Compasses the exquisite skill of Hiram Abiff; but the truly speculative Mason regards them as the unerring standards of the wisdom, truth and justice of the Most High, His wisdom is amply exemplified in the Volume of the Sacred Law, which contains the record of His mighty acts, and is the register of His revealed will. His truth is justly depicted by the Square, that being the acknowledged symbol of strength and criterion of perfection, while His unerring and impartial justice in having defined for our instruction the limits of good and evil, assigning to each his due proportion of pleasure and pain, is elucidated by the Compasses, by which instrument we are enabled to ascertain and determine the limits and proportions of all geometrical figures, and reduce our ideas of their proportion and equality to a given standard.

The Sword and Trowel were adopted by Royal Arch Masons to commemorate the valour of those worthy men who assisted at the building of the second Temple, who with Trowel in their hand and Sword by their side were ever ready to defend the City and Holy Sanctuary against the unprovoked attacks of their enemies, thereby leaving an impressive lesson to future ages, that next to implicit obedience to all lawfully constituted authority, a manly and determined resistance to lawless violence is the first step in social duty. The Pickaxe, Crowbar, and Shovel were the implements made use of by the Sojourners who were sent to prepare the ground for the foundation of the second Temple. The Pick to loosen the ground, the Crow to take purchases, and the Shovel to clear away the rubbish and loose earth. These we spiritualize. The stroke of the Pick reminds us of the sound of the last trumpet, when the ground shall be shaken, and loosened, and the graves deliver up their dead; the Crow being an emblem of uprightness, points to the erect manner in which the body shall rise on that awful day to meet its tremendous though merciful Judge; while the manner in which the body is laid in the grave is fully depicted by the work of the Shovel, and we, with humble but holy confidence, hope that when these earthly remains shall have been properly disposed of, the spirit will arise to immortal life and everlasting bliss.

The principals give the four knocks.

The address of the First Chair—the Mystical Lecture

Z.   Companions, the mystical knowledge of this Degree comprehends the forms and explanation of the Sacred Signs, the nature and import of the Holy Words, and the traditional ceremonies to be observed in sharing and communicating our secrets. In Royal Arch Masonry we acknowledge five signs, corresponding in number with the Five Points of Fellowship, in which the Master Mason has already been instructed; and as these point out the relative duties we owe to each other, so do the former signs mark, in a peculiar manner, the relation we bear to the Most High as creatures offending against His mighty will and power, yet still the adopted children of His mercy.

Zerubbabel hands his sceptre to Joshua, rises and says to Candidate:

Z.   I will now go through the signs, and you, my newly exalted Companion, will rise and copy me. This is the Penal sign, the only perfect sign in Freemasonry given with the left hand. This is the Reverential or Hailing sign, and is to be used on all occasions when entering or retiring from the Chapter, or when addressing the Principals. This is the Penitential or Supplicatory sign, on bended knees and with uplifted hands. This is the Monitorial, hands girding the loins, thumbs in front, and this is the Fiducial sign. You will now resume your seats, and I will explain them at greater length.

The Penal sign marks the penalty of our Obligation, and alludes to the fall of Adam, and the dreadful penalty entailed thereby of his sinful posterity, no less than death. It intimates by the very act that the stiff-necked and disobedient shall be cut off from the land of the living by the judgment of God, even as the head is severed from the body by the sword of human justice.

To avert which, we are taught by the Reverential or Hailing sign to bend with humility and resignation beneath the chastening hand of the Almighty, at the same time to engraft His laws on our hearts. In this expressive form did the father of the human race present himself before the Most High, to receive the enunciation of his just though terrible doom; and this sign was afterwards adopted by our Grand Master Moses, who, when the Lord appeared to him in the burning bush, at the foot of Mount Horeb in the wilderness of Sinai, thus shielded his eyes from the brightness of the Divine presence, and placed his hand on his heart in token of obedience, and this sign was afterwards accounted unto him for righteousness.

The Reverential or Hailing sign may justly be deemed the parent of the Penitential or Supplicatory sign, since it so truly denotes that frame of heart and mind without which our prayers and oblations of praise cannot find acceptance at the throne of grace, before which how should a frail and erring creature of the dust present himself but on bended knees and with uplifted hands, at once betokening his humility and contrition? Thus did Adam kneel to God, and bless the Author of his being; thus too did he bend with contrite awe before the face of his offended Judge, to avert His wrath and propitiate His mercy, and has transmitted this outward form of humility and contrition to his posterity for ever.

The Monitorial sign reminds us of the weakness of human nature, unable of itself to resist the powers of darkness, unless assisted by that light which is from above. By this defenceless posture we acknowledge our whole frailty, and confess that we can do no manner of good or acceptable service but through Him from whom all good counsels and just works do proceed, and without whose Divine and special favour we must ever have remained unprofitable servants in His sight.

Therefore, after the manner of our holy ancestors, the atoning priests by this outward form of faith and dependence, the Fiducial sign, we show that we would prostrate ourselves with our faces to the dust. Thus must we throw ourselves on the mercy of our Divine Creator and Judge, looking forward with humble but holy confidence to His blessed promises, by which means alone we hope to pass through the ark of redemption into the mansions of eternal bliss and glory, into the presence of Him who is the great I AM, the Alpha and Omega, the beginning and the end, the first and the last.

At the building of King Solomon's Temple, a vast number of Masons were employed, and their names or marks were found engraven on some part or other of the building, but the names of the three Grand Masters who presided were nowhere found, until they were discovered in the Royal Arch by the Sojourners, who were sent to prepare the ground for the foundation of the second Temple. In the centre of the Vault stood a block of white marble, wrought in the form of the Altar of Incense, a double cube, on the top of which was a plate of gold, white being an emblem of innocence, and gold of purity. On the front were engraven the initials of the three Grand Masters who presided at the building of the former Temple, that is, Solomon King of Israel, Hiram King of Tyre, and Hiram Abiff, and were meant to perpetuate their names as well as to commemorate the circumstance and proceedings attending the erection of that structure. There was likewise the mysterious triple tau, a mark or character affixed to the summonses of Royal Arch Masons, on occasions of more than usual importance. The tau is derived from the Hebrew, and is that mark or sign spoken of by the angel whom Ezekiel saw in the spirit, when it was said to the man with the writer's ink horn: 'Go through the midst of the city, through the midst of Jerusalem, and set a mark upon the foreheads of the men that sigh and that cry for all the abominations that be done in the midst thereof,' by which mark they were saved from among those who were slain for their idolatry by the wrathful displeasure of the Most High. In ancient times, this mark was placed upon those who were acquitted by their judges in proof of their innocence, and military commanders caused it to be set on the foreheads of the men who returned unhurt from the field of battle, denoting that they were in perfect life. For these reasons it has ever been considered a mark or sign of life. The union of the taus, here depicted, alludes to the Deity, by whom the gloomy, horrific, and unshapen chaos was changed into regular form and peaceful existence.

Zerubbabel returns to the east side of the altar, Candidate is brought up by the Sojourner to the south side.

Z.   On this plate of gold are a circle and a triangle; these mathematical figures have ever been selected as referring to the Deity or some Divine attribute. The circle is an emblem of eternity, for as it has neither beginning nor end it may justly be deemed a type of God, without beginning of days or end of years, and it continually reminds us of that great hereafter, when we hope to enjoy endless life, and everlasting bliss. The word on the circle is JEHOVAH, that great, awful, tremendous and incomprehensible Name of the Most High. It signifies I Am that I Am, the Alpha and Omega, the beginning and the end, the first and the last, who was, and is, and is to come, the Almighty. It is the name of the actual, future, eternal, unchangeable, and all-sufficient God, who alone has His being in and from Himself, and gives to all others their being; so that He is what He was, was what He is, and will remain both what He was, and what He is, from everlasting to everlasting, all creatures being dependent on His mighty will and power.

    As previously observed, on top of the Pedestal should be a plate of pure gold, with a circle and a triangle of the same material. The selection of these mathematical figures has ever had a reference to the Deity, or some Divine attribute. From the most remote period of antiquity, names of God and symbols of Deity were always enclosed in triangular figures. In the days of Pythagoras, the triangle was considered the most sacred of emblems, and when any obligation of more than usual importance was to be administered, it was invariably given on the Triangle, and when so taken, none were ever known to violate it. The Egyptians termed it the sacred number, or number of perfection, and so highly was it prized by the ancients, that it became amongst them an object of worship. Under the principles of animated nature they gave it the sacred name of God, affirming that it represented the animal, mineral, and vegetable kingdoms; they also called it Abroeth, which signifies Soul of Nature. This Sacred Delta is usually enclosed with a square and circle, thereby expressing its vivifying influence, extending its ramifications through all created nature; for these reasons it has ever been considered the Great All, the Summum Bonum.

The word on the triangle is that Sacred and Mysterious Name you have solemnly engaged yourself never to pronounce, unless in the presence and with the assistance of two or more Royal Arch Companions, or in the body of a lawfully-constituted Royal Arch Chapter, whilst acting as First Principal. It is a compound word, and the combination forms the word JAH-BUL-ON. It is in four languages, Chaldee, Hebrew, Syriac, and Egyptian. JAH is the Chaldee name of God, signifying 'His Essence in Majesty Incomprehensible'. It is also a Hebrew word, signifying 'I am and shall be', thereby expressing the actual, future and eternal existence of the Most High. BUL is a Syriac word signifying Lord or Powerful. It is in itself a compound word, being formed from the preposition Beth, in or on, and Ul, Heaven, or on High; therefore the meaning of the word is Lord in Heaven, or on High. ON is an Egyptian word, signifying

Father of all, thereby expressing the Omnipotence of the Father of All, as in that well-known prayer, Our Father, which art in Heaven. The various significations of the words may be thus collected: I am and shall be; Lord in Heaven or on High: 'Father of All! In every age, In every clime adored By saint, by savage, and by sage, Jehovah, Jove, or Lord.'

The characters at the angles of the Triangle are of exceeding importance, though it is immaterial where the combination is commenced, as each has reference to the Deity of some Divine attribute. They are the Aleph, the Beth, and the Lamed of the Hebrew, corresponding with the A., B., and L. of the English alphabet. Take the Aleph and the Beth, they form the word AB, which is Father; take the Beth, the Aleph, and the Lamed, they form BAL, which is Lord; take the Aleph and the Lamed, they form AL, which is Word; take the Lamed, the Aleph, and the Beth, they form LAB, which signifies Heart or Spirit. Take each combination with the whole, and it will read thus: AB BAL, Father, Lord; AL BAL, Word, Lord; LAB BAL, Spirit, Lord.

Such, my newly exalted Companion, is the best explanation I can give of those sacred words and characters; it proves the Royal Arch to be the climax of Freemasonry, and is so intimately blended with all that is nearest and dearest to us in a future state of existence: Divine and human affairs are interwoven so awfully and minutely in all its disquisitions. It has virtue for its aim, the glory of God for its object, and the eternal welfare of man is considered in every part, point, and letter of its ineffable mysteries. Suffice it to say, it is founded on the Sacred Name, Jehovah (or 'of God') who was from all beginning, is now, and will remain one and the same for ever, the Being necessarily existing in and from Himself in all actual perfection, original in His essence.

Companions, I charge you, should you ever be about to mention that Sacred and Mysterious Name lightly or irreverently, pause, place your finger on your lips, and remember the penalty of your Obligation.

This Supreme Degree inspires its members with the most exalted ideas of God, and leads to the exercise of the purest and most devout piety, a reverence for the incomprehensible JEHOVAH, the eternal Ruler of the Universe, the elemental life and primordial source of all its principles, the very spring and fount of all its virtues.

The Ceremony of closing a Royal Arch Chapter

Z. *(knocks)* I rise for the first time to enquire if any companion has aught to propose for the good of Royal Arch Masonry in general, or this Chapter in particular?

This is repeated two or three times.

Z. Companions assist me to close the Chapter.

They repeat as in the opening.

Z.H. We do all meet and agree . . . in love and unity . . . the
and J. Sacred Word to keep . . . and never to divulge the same . . . unless when three . . . such as we (. . . or 'Three such as we') . . . do meet and agree . . . agree (Z) . . . agree (H) . . . agree (J) . . . agree (Z).

The Principals salute the Volume, which is then closed and they form a triangle with their sceptres

Z. Companion Principal Sojourner, the labours of this convocation being ended, you have my command to close the Chapter. *(Knocks)*

P.S. Companions, in the name of the True and Living God Most High, and by command of the Most Excellent, I close this Chapter until . . . emergencies excepted, of which every Companion will have due notice.

Z. Glory to God in the highest.

H. On earth peace.

J. Goodwill towards men.

P.Z. Companions, nothing now remains but, according to

ancient custom, to lock up our secrets in a safe repository, uniting in the act fidelity, fidelity, fidelity, fidelity.

Zerubbabel disarranges letters on plate while speaking. At
each repetition of the word 'fidelity' the Fiducial sign is given.

[End of closing Royal Arch Chapter].

Notes

Introduction
1. C. Penney Hunt, *The Menace of Freemasonry to the Christian Faith*, 5th ed., pp.6-7.
2. S. Knight, *The Brotherhood*.

Chapter 1
1. W. Hannah, *Darkness Visible, Christian by Degrees*.

Chapter 2
1. See chapter 10 note 1.
2. *Aims and Relationships of the Craft,* accepted by Grand Lodge, September 7th 1949, para 4, contained in Information for the Guidance of Members of the Craft (a copy of which is given to all initiates).
3. The *Aims and Relationships of the Craft,* which appeared in 1949, state that no mason would be permitted 'to discuss or to advance his views on theological or political questions' in any lodge.
4. *General Laws and Regulations* No. 30. See *Constitutions 1970*.

Chapter 3

1. D. Knoop and G. P. Jones, *A Short History of Free-masonry to 1730,* Introduction, p.(v).
2. F. L. Pick and G. N. Knight, *Antiquities of Freemasonry,* p.26.
3. F. L. Pick and G. N. Knight, *The Pocket History of Freemasonry,* 6th ed., p.18.
4. A. Mellor, *Our Separated Brethren—The Freemasons,* p. 57.
5. D. Knoop and G. P. Jones, op. cit. p.74.
6. F. L. Pick and G. N. Knight, *The Pocket History of Freemasonry,* 6th ed. pp.76-77.
7. A. Cowan, *X-Rays in Freemasonry,* pp.44-46.
8. A. Cowan, ibid. pp.25-26.
9. J. S. M. Ward, *Higher Degrees Handbook,* p.3f.
10. J. S. M. Ward, ibid, p.4.
11. H. G. M. Clarke, *Freemasonry and Religion,* contained in *Grand Lodge 1717-1967,* Appendix A p.213.
12. A. Cowan, op.cit. pp.59-60.
13. A. Cowan, ibid. p.60.
14. Folger, *History of the A and A Scottish Rite* (New York, 1863) p.93.

Chapter 4

1. Quoted in A. Mellor, *Our Separated Brethren,* pp.159-160.
2. Humanum Genus—Encyclical Letter of His Holiness Pope Leo XIII on Freemasonry, April 20th 1884 (Tan Books) pp.3-4.
3. ibid, p.9.
4. ibid, pp.5, 19.
5. M. Dumesnil de Gramont, *La Maconnerie et L'Eglise Catholique* p.18. Translated by T. Tindal-Robertson in *Freemasonry and the Vatican* p.33 (de Poncins).
6. L. de Poncins, *Freemasonry and the Vatican,* p.34.

7. L. de Poncins, ibid. p.13.
8. H. Carr, *The Freemason at Work,* p.281.
9. H. Carr, ibid. p.281.
10. Declaration of the Sacred Congregation for Doctrine of the Faith—19th July 1974 see *Freemasonry for Beginners and Others*—A. L. Philips p.83.
11. *The German Bishops on Freemasonry* translation by Rev. William Lawson S. J. pp.5-6.
12. ibid. p.12.
13. See *The Tablet,* December 10th 1983.

Chapter 5
1. C. Penney Hunt, *The Menace of Freemasonry to the Christian Faith,* introduction.
2. Quoted in C. Penney Hunt, ibid. pp.92-93.
3. The report of the Faith and Order Committee presented to the Methodist Conference July 3rd 1985.
4. *Methodist Recorder* July 11th 1985, p.1.
5. W. Hannah, *Darkness Visible,* p.78.
6. W. Hannah, ibid. p.75-6.
7. W. Hannah, ibid. p.73.

Chapter 6
1. F. L. Pick and G. N. Knight, *The Pocket History of Freemasonry,* 6th ed., p.130.
2. W. Hannah, *Darkness Visible,* pp.46-47.
3. *Church of England Newspaper,* July 6th 1962.
4. F. L. Pick and G. N. Knight, *Pocket History of Freemasonry,* p.131.
5. *Grand Lodge 1717-1967,* pp.200-201.
6. *Church Times,* June 29th 1951.
7. M. Stockwood, *Chanctonbury Ring,* pp.113-114.
8. *Church of England Newspaper* July 6th 1962.
9. W. Hannah, *Christian by Degrees,* p.7.
10. Article in *Life of Faith,* October 15th 1952.

11. Conducted by Ralph Jones for the London Weekend Television *Credo* series May 1981, in connection with a programme on Freemasonry and the Church TX June 28th 1981.
12. *The Times,* February 27th 1976.

Chapter 7
1. All masonic rituals contain coded abbreviation. For example: 'W.M.—This word is derived from the l.h.p. at the p . . . way of K.S.T. . . . .' This is a quotation by the W.M. (Worshipful Master) who says, 'This word is derived from the left hand pillar at the porchway of King Solomon's Temple . . . .'

 If different rituals are compared it can be seen that there is no uniform system of abbreviation. I have several masonic rituals as well as various independently produced complete texts, as well as consulting with several past and present masons to confirm the accuracy of my quotations. No one ritual is definitive, so I have sought to quote the most commonly used words since there are minor differences in all rituals.
2. Isaiah 64:6.
3. C. Penney Hunt, op.cit. p.30.
4. Isaiah 55:8; 64:6.
5. J. S. M. Ward, *Second Degree Handbook* p.68.
6. W. Hannah, *Darkness Visible,* 13th ed., p.131.
7. Revelation 22:18-19.

Chapter 8
1. See chapter 2 note 1.
2. W. Hannah, *Christian by Degrees,* p.99.
3. See chapter 9 of W. Hannah, *Christian by Degrees.*
4. W. Hannah, *Darkness Visible,* pp.206-207.
5. W. Hannah, *Christian by Degrees,* p.136.

Chapter 9.
1. *Grand Lodge 1717-1967,* p.201.
2. BBC Radio 4 'Sunday' programme TX June 15th 1985.
3. J. Cockburn, *Freemasonry, What, Whence, Why, Whither* (Masonic Record Ltd) quoted in *Darkness Visible,* p.31.

Chapter 10
1. *Constitutions,* 1970 — U.G.L. p.3.
2. M. Higham, *A Christian in the Technological Age,* p.4.
3. 2 Corinthians 6:15-17.

Chapter 11
1. J. Johnson, *The Lure of Freemasonry* (Masonic Record Ltd).

Chapter 12
1. W. J. McCormick, *Christ, the Christian and Freemasonry* (B. McCall Barbour, Edinburgh).

Further Recommended Reading

Carr, Harry, *The Freemason at Work* (A. Lewis Masonic, 1981).

De Pace, M., *Introducing Freemasonry* (A. Lewis Masonic, 1983).

De Poncins, Leon, *Freemasonry and the Vatican* (Britons Publishing, 1968).

Hannah, Walton, *Christian by Degrees* (Britons Publishing, 1954).

Hannah, Walton, *Darkness Visible* (Britons Publishing, 1975).

Hunt, C. Penney, *The Menace of Freemasonry to the Christian Faith* (Freedom Press, Breaston, Derby, 1934).

Jackson, Keith B., *Beyond the Craft* (A. Lewis Masonic, 1982).

Knight, Stephen, *The Brotherhood* (Granada, 1983).

Lawrence, John, *Freemasonry—A Way of Salvation?* (Grove Books, Bramcote, Notts., 1985).

Philips, A. L., *Freemasonry for Beginners—and Others* (R.M.B.I. Services, second edition 1976).

Pick, F. L. & Knight, G. N., *The Pocket History of Free-*

masonry (Muller, sixth edition 1977).

Stockwood, Mervyn, *Chanctonbury Ring: An Autobiography* (Sheldon/Hodder & Stoughton, 1982).

Various, Grand Lodge 1717-1967 (United Grand Lodge of England 1967).

Guidance to Methodists on Freemasonry. The report of the Faith and Order Committee presented to the Methodist Conference on 3rd July 1985.

The German Bishops on Freemasonry. A translation of the statement published by the German Episcopal Conference in April 1980 by the Rev. William Lawson, S.J. (Supplement to 'Approaches' No.74) from 1 Waverley Place, Saltcoats, Ayrshire KA21 5AX, Scotland.

Humanum Genus. Encyclical letter of His Holiness Pope Leo XIII on Freemasonry, April 20, 1884. Tan Books & Publishers Inc., P.O. Box 424, Rockford, Illinois 61105, U.S.A.

Other Books Used

Cowan, A., *X-rays in Freemasonry* (Effingham Wilson, 1901).

Higham, Michael, *A Christian in a Technological Age, Freemasonry—from Craft to Tolerance*. Obtainable from: United Grand Lodge, Great Queen Street, London WC2B 5AZ.

Johnson, Joseph, *The Lure of Freemasonry* (Masonic Record Ltd).

Knoop, D. and Jones, G. P., *A Short History of Freemasonry* (Manchester Univ. Press, 1940).

Mellor, Alec, *Our Separated Brethren: The Freemasons* (Harrap, 1964).

Ward, J. S. M., *Higher Degrees Handbook* (Baskerville).

Constitutions: United Grand Lodge of England (1970), including a summary of the Ancient Charges, and the General Laws and Regulations for the government of the Craft.

Freemason's Hall, Official Guide Book.

Information for the Guidance of Members of the Craft,

including Aims & Relationships of the Craft, accepted by G.L. 1949 and Basic Principles for Grand Lodge Recognition (1929), together with Points of Procedure—recommendations adopted by Grand Lodge, 1916-76.

Masonic Year Book. Annual list of Craft & Royal Arch officials together with list of Grand, Provincial and Oversees lodges and much other information.

The above four publications are published by the United Grand Lodge of England, Freemasons' Hall, Great Queen Street, WC2B 5AZ.